BEYOND
mile marker 80

FOREWORD BY CHAD HYMAS

BEYOND
mile marker 80

CHOOSING JOY
AFTER
TRAGIC LOSS

JEFF OLSEN

PLAIN SIGHT PUBLISHING
AN IMPRINT OF CEDAR FORT, INC.
SPRINGVILLE, UTAH

ISBN 13: 978-1-4621-1398-9

Published by Plain Sight Publishing, an imprint of Cedar Fort, Inc.
2373 W. 700 S., Springville, UT 84663
Distributed by Cedar Fort, Inc., www.cedarfort.com

LIBRARY OF CONGRESS CATALOGING-IN-PUBLICATION DATA

Olsen, Jeff, 1964- author.
Beyond mile marker 80 / Jeffery C. Olsen.
      pages cm
Summary: Memoir describing the author's bereavement following the death of his wife and small child and the new family he later forms.
ISBN 978-1-4621-1398-9 (alk. paper)
1. Olsen, Jeff, 1964- 2. Bereavement--Religious aspects--Church of Jesus Christ of Latter-day Saints. 3. Autobiographies. I. Title.

BX8643.D4O47 2014
289.3092--dc23
[B]

                                        2014001485

Cover design by Angela Baxter
Cover design © 2014 by Lyle Mortimer
Edited and typeset by Deborah Spencer

Printed in the United States of America

10 9 8 7 6 5 4 3 2 1

Printed on acid-free paper

For Mom and Dad, who love us, unconditionally, every step of the way.

contents

contents

foreword

What an inspiring journey Jeff takes us on. In *I Knew Their Hearts*, Olsen's account of the accident that caused the loss of his wife and toddler son is traumatic, but the story is not one of tragedy. It's not even really a tale of triumph at its core, but rather a witness to the creation of heroes. Nobody ever promised us that life is fair for the simple reason that it isn't. We simply get to cope with the hand we are dealt and turn our weaknesses into strengths. This is what Jeff Olsen has done with his life as he shares in this book.

When one small decision resulted in a life-changing accident, Jeff could have stayed lost in despair—and was, at times, tempted to. But—with love, support, and inspiration from family and friends—he turned his life around and moved toward new choices: to live, to love, to thrive, to inspire. *Beyond Mile Marker 80* is an incredible story of perseverance, perspective, and finding purpose and passion. It belongs on your must-read list. Your life will be forever touched because of Jeff's honest, candid, and heartfelt words as he shares his remarkable experience with us.

For those who think their trial, problem, or trauma is too hard to bear, Jeff will take you on a spiritual journey to heal your heart. Jeff takes us through his valley of despair, and as he does so we have the opportunity to evaluate our own lives. You will find yourself thinking, "How would I handle this? Would I act or react? Would I give up or look up? Would I throw in the towel or would I give it one more day, week, or month? Would I notice my small successes or give up when things seemed impossible?" Jeff will invite you into a deep state of self-reflection. How often have you shied away, backed off, or flat out given up because a situation or goal was too daunting? And here's someone with every justifiable reason in the world to give up, yet he's doing the impossible. *Beyond Mile Marker 80* will make you feel, think, weep, and laugh. It will also cause you to realize something you've never considered before—there is a "gift in injury." We just have to find it.

In a long list of achievements in Jeff's life, including the many awards he has received and becoming a successful and loving husband and father, writing this book is just one of a long string of victories hard won, with many more yet to come.

As you read within, please be willing to open up your heart. Consider those in your circle of influence, and those you have yet to meet, and then leave these pages with a greater desire, and let your journey find its destiny! Take notes throughout. Write down your thoughts. Act on instinct. Then watch the transformation unfold! What has come to fruition in the last decade of the author's life is nothing shy of a miracle. I sincerely wish the same results for you in your life.

—*Chad Hymas*
CPAE Award Recipient,
Inductee, National Speaker Hall of Fame

acknowledgments

To my sons: Thank you for inspiring me to be a better man.
To Tonya: Thank you for teaching me unconditional love.
To my brothers: Thank you for showing up for me in the perfect
    way, every time.
To my little sisters: Thank you for your depth of character.
To Mom: Thank you for listening.
To Dad: Thank you for making me strong.
To Hans and Sally: Thank you for holding the context.
To my angels: Thank you for profound insights and answers.
To my heart: Thank you for healing.

introduction

I once read a story about a potter who would create beautiful pots. He would glaze them with fantastic finishes, only to wrap them in burlap and break them into hundreds of pieces. Then he would meticulously reassemble the pieces back together, filling the cracks with contrasting colors. When asked why he did such a thing, he explained that the process made each pot unique. It made them interesting and gave them character.

At mile marker 80—about two and a half hours north of Las Vegas—I was shattered. I lost my wife, my youngest son, my left leg, and nearly my own life in a horrific automobile accident.

How does one reassemble a life? Mine had been crushed into so many pieces I felt I could never find them all, let alone put them back together.

I was sure I was losing my mind as I did my best to find "normal" again. Raising my surviving son, Spencer, alone was a challenge. Being productive at work and masking my grief was a battle. Dealing with my physical injuries after eighteen surgeries and a year of rehabilitation was still an uphill climb. I'd had profound spiritual experiences over the past twelve months, but I was still healing.

We never recognize how much support we receive. At least I didn't. I waded through the mayhem barely holding on, but in hindsight, I see how many angels came to assist me in putting it back together. Some were family, friends, and neighbors. Others were very much from a heavenly realm, but they came to heal, to guide, to comfort, and to direct. I learned how to listen, to trust, and to find peace. Eventually I recognized the miracles that had been so evident in my life—the biggest being that I finally decided to choose joy even in difficult circumstances, and that made all the difference.

I've often wondered if our lives are like those pots. Perhaps only when we are shattered and then reassembled do we step into our true glory as one of God's masterpieces.

chapter 1

Inhale.

I took a deep breath and felt my chest rise and expand. After all the trauma my lungs had been through, effortlessly taking air in felt good. With the pulmonary embolisms, the life-threatening bouts with pneumonia, and the injuries my ribs and chest had sustained in the accident, breathing without pain or coughing was beyond liberating.

I exhaled and opened my eyes, focusing out the open bedroom window onto the wild grasses that had begun to sprout up on the back hill. I took another deep breath and came into full consciousness. Mornings were the most difficult. I believed I would eventually wake up from the nightmare; however, the light coming in from the small east-facing window reminded me that the nightmare was my reality. I took another deep breath and looked at the long shadows created by the light coming into the room. This morning felt different, welcoming. I felt alive—which I hadn't felt since the accident. I leaned up on my left arm to take another look at the back hill. I felt distanced from all the pain, as if today I were only observing my life rather than living it. It was a refreshing reprieve from the normal routine of opening my eyes, yet again, to the emptiness of what had happened. It had been almost a year since the accident. I had experienced so much grief and regret over those long months I believed it would never end. Yet this morning was different. The air smelled of Russian olive trees and was filled with the still energy of spring, the electric anticipation of rebirth. I heard birds singing.

I sat up and swung my leg out of bed. I felt the coolness of the floor as I stood up, bracing myself on the nightstand to reach for my crutches. I felt as if I were taking my first steps. I paused, steadying myself for a moment and looked about the room. I saw reminders of my little son Griffin and my late wife, Tamara. Griffin's small handprints were still on the full-length mirror in the closet, and Tamara's sweater was still neatly laid over the chair next to the bed, just as she had left it the day before the accident. I couldn't bring myself to clean the mirror or move that sweater. Leaving them there allowed me to feel closer to them. I had grieved for so long—yet today, I felt their presence stronger than ever.

I felt my lungs expand with life again as I breathed in the spring air, placed my crutches under my arms, and hobbled on my one leg toward the shower. The water felt invigorating on my chest and on the back of my neck. I felt gratitude as I dried off, put on my prosthetic leg, and dressed for the day. Driving into the city felt brighter. I turned on music. Even walking with my cane into the office that morning felt easier. My desk seemed to greet me; the energy of having work to do felt good. I popped into coworkers' offices to say hello. They invited me to join them for lunch at a fancy restaurant we'd been invited to. They were all discussing it and making plans. I declined, but as they insisted, spring and their warm beckoning became so welcoming I could not refuse. What was it about this day that felt so different? The pain and grief were far from gone but now seemed numbed by the energy that had surrounded me from the time I opened my eyes. The hours rolled along easy and simply embraced me. Every event of that morning, even letting my coworkers convince me to go to that fancy luncheon meeting, had led up to a very powerful right now.

chapter 2

There I was at the luncheon. I sat across from a stranger, still engulfed in my new feelings of the day. I watched as she cut her steak into small, bite-sized pieces. She was delicate but deliberate. I first noticed her hands. They were feminine but no stranger to hard work. Her nails weren't false or fancy but well kept. I looked at her trim, fit arms as she sawed at the steak, cutting several small pieces at a time before she'd dip one into the silver relish dish of ketchup on her plate and put it into her mouth. *Ketchup, on a USDA Prime Choice New York strip?* I found it strange and amusing yet somehow endearing.

"Hi, my name is Jeff," I said politely and reached across the table to shake her hand. She put down her fork and took my hand with a firm but feminine handshake.

"I'm Tonya," she replied. "Pleased to meet you."

We returned to our meals and sat in awkward silence for a few brief seconds before I remembered her mentioning she was not from here in the short presentation she gave before sitting down.

"So how long have you been in Utah?" I asked her as I swallowed and wiped the corner of my mouth with the white linen napkin.

"Not long," she replied. "And yet long enough. I'm not sure I like it here. In fact, I'm leaving soon to live with my sister in Arizona. I'll be making the official announcement today at this luncheon. I intend to move as soon as next month."

"Wow. At least you'll be moving to warmer weather," I remarked.

"Yes, and new possibilities. I came out here for work—and for a guy—but things haven't worked out. And Utah's strange. It's been difficult meeting people here. You either have to be in a bar or at church, and I'm not necessarily comfortable in either place."

She dipped another small piece of steak in ketchup and bit it off the fork with her teeth so as to not smear her lipstick. She lifted her hand to cover her mouth while she chewed and asked, "What do you do?"

"Oh, lots of things I guess. By day I'm a creative director at a local ad agency. At night, however, I transform into a single dad." I paused. The words were still painful to say, even after a year. Verbalizing it brought the pain of what had happened to the surface.

"I was widowed a year ago. I'm still working to find 'normal' I guess."

She stopped chewing, swallowed hard, and looked at me. "I'm sorry," she said.

I shook my head. "It's not your fault."

I always felt the sting of my own remorse whenever someone said, "I'm sorry." I was driving the car when my wife and toddler son were killed in the accident. No one felt as sorry as I did.

I watched again as she cut more small pieces from the steak. I noticed again—in slow motion—all the details of her hands, arms, and face as I began to have the strangest déjà vu. I looked at her eyes. Memories of the first time I met Tamara, my late wife, came rushing over me.

I had an overwhelming feeling like this the first time I saw her. I was young, only a junior in college, but this same striking jolt that was rushing through me now had happened nearly thirteen years earlier when I first encountered Tamara—the rush of seeing her sky-blue eyes as she pulled her blonde bangs back to look at me for the first time. I recalled her smile, her soft confidence, that feeling of floating and yet being more solidly planted on the ground than ever before. I remembered the way she smelled and how my soul seemed to jump at simply catching her glance. I recalled the feeling of those warm goose bumps down the small of my back and that sense of knowing a secret, but I wasn't sure what it was. And here it was all rushing over me again. I immersed myself in the familiar recollection, but why was I feeling such things? Was it the conversation and admitting I was widowed? I wasn't sure, but I felt that same intense tingle of "knowing" all over again.

I glanced back up at the woman sitting across from me, who was scooping vegetables onto her fork. Perhaps she looked like Tamara, at least a little bit. Maybe that's what took me so much by surprise. I sat silently, staring at her. She had the same stunning blue eyes, but she projected a new feeling altogether. She was foreign yet familiar, kind yet driven. She had the same physical build as Tamara but was unique in every way. Everything around her seemed to darken, and it looked as if she were sitting under a spotlight. What was going on? Why was this happening? It wasn't like I hadn't sat with or spoken to other women over those long lonely months. I had! So why did I have all these feelings now? And why was it so similar to the first time I met my late wife?

I'm losing it! I thought to myself. *I really must be going crazy. This woman—a stranger—sits across from me, and I can't even concentrate on the conversation because of all the emotions flooding over me.*

I quickly changed the subject. "How's the steak?" I asked.

"Good, actually. The best I've had in a long time," she replied.

She looked up at me. I noticed her stunning blue eyes again, and felt another deep ping in my core. She stabbed another small piece of steak with her fork, swirled it into the dish of ketchup, and popped it into her mouth, this time paying no mind to her lipstick. She too gracefully swept her bangs aside to look at me.

"How long have you been in advertising?" she continued as she chewed on the steak. I could tell she wanted to escape the widower topic and find much more comfortable ground to tread on, avoiding the real questions she wanted to ask. How many children did I have? How was I widowed? What happened? I'm sure she also felt my anxiety about the topic and purposely kept things at shallow small talk for my sake.

"Over ten years now," I answered. "I started right out of college, and it's all I've ever done."

I did my best to push away the overwhelming yet familiar feelings and finished my food. At this point, I simply wanted to escape these strange emotions and get back to the office. It was too much to take in. I wiped my mouth again with the napkin and pushed back my chair. "It was a pleasure meeting you," I said, gripping my cane to find my balance as I stood up on my prosthetic leg. "Thank you for sitting by me." I reached out to shake her hand. "Here's to Salt Lake City treating you better the rest of your stay here."

"Yes, thank you," she said as she reached down beside her chair into her bag to pull out a business card. She handed me the card and smiled. "Call me if you need any specifications on designer paper or samples of any kind."

"Will do," I replied as I took the card and smiled back at her.

I turned and walked away, wondering whether she noticed my limp as I did so. I was doing my best to let go of the overwhelming feelings I'd been having. *Why do I care?* I felt awkward, and the whole ordeal had put me in a bit of a funk.

I began locating my work associates as they mingled and said their good-byes. I looked back, one more time, at the woman I'd just met and felt that same bolt of recognition that was so hauntingly familiar. I shook my head and continued limping to the reception area to wait for the others.

I looked at the business card she'd handed me. "Tonya Skubic," I said under my breath, rubbing my thumb over the raised letters on the thick paper. I put the card in my pocket and decided to make my way to the parking garage. I was still learning to walk on the artificial limb and wanted to take my time so I wouldn't fall or lose my balance. I stumbled often and didn't want to cause a scene in front of the lunch crowd. I easily made it to my truck and began driving back toward the office. *I probably should have stayed behind and not gone to lunch*, I thought as I made the turn into our office parking lot, still wondering why I had felt so strongly toward Tonya and why she was still lingering on my mind. *I definitely do not get out enough*, I figured as I parked and made my way back to my desk.

chapter 3

It was almost two when I sat down and looked at my computer screen. I had plenty to do and didn't want the extended lunch break to put me further behind in getting home to my eight-year-old. The workday took over, and soon it was after six. I knew my son Spencer would be waiting at home, so I put the day's unfinished layouts aside and headed to the parking lot to get into my truck. Spring was still in the air and as powerful with energy as it had been for me that morning. The sun was starting to set, but it was still warm enough that I felt the heat of its low rays on my shoulders as I crossed the street to the parking lot.

I enjoyed driving again. I had purchased a truck after the accident because I found that stepping up into a truck with my one leg was much easier than bending down to sit in a lower-profile car. I'd been driving for a few months now, and it was liberating to be out of a wheelchair, to learn to walk, and to be independent enough to not rely on family and friends for transportation. I had worried about getting behind the wheel again. The memory of the accident was still painful. But it was an important step in my recovery, and at this point driving had become natural again. The fear of the crash had subsided. I reached up to switch on the radio, but I still could not lift my right arm high enough to press the knob. My arm had been nearly torn off in the accident. The entire rotator cuff had been detached. There had also been large lacerations on the upper arm, which caused nerve damage. I let go of the wheel briefly to use my left arm to assist my right arm to the height of the radio switch on the dash. I was even okay with letting go of the wheel for a brief second.

As I drove home, I reflected on the day and the woman I had met, but my thoughts quickly refocused on Spencer as soon as I parked and came into the house. When I came through the door to greet him, he was enjoying a large bowl of macaroni and cheese that the nanny had made for him. We reviewed the day's homework, and then we both sat in the big recliner in the front room to watch television for a while before bed.

I was thankful that Spencer seemed to be doing so well, but there was still a sadness and emptiness in our home since it had become just the two of us. We had developed a routine, which covered the dull sting of it all. We sat together a lot and did things to keep us occupied every night until it was time to sleep. Then I would put him to bed and enter into the thick silence of the house, dealing with my own lingering emotions.

With everything quiet and Spencer sleeping, I made my way up the stairs to my bedroom. It still took a bit to navigate the stairs with my artificial leg, but I was getting better. I just had to concentrate on taking one step at a time and make sure I had the false leg securely under me before I took the next step up. I'd never really noticed the sturdy handrails before the accident, but I was glad they were there now to assist me.

As I sat on the bed and took off my prosthesis, I wondered if I would ever feel whole again. I had experienced so many powerful, spiritual things over the long months of my physical recovery, but I still had far to go. As I undressed, I looked at the stump that once was my leg and all the scars on my body. A lot of things had changed for me, but I was adapting to my new life. I reflected again on the woman I'd met at lunch that day, Tonya. Why did she linger on my mind? I looked at the sweater Tamara had left on the chair next to the bed. Would I ever have the courage to put it away? I reached down over the side of the bed to my clothes lying on the floor. I took out the business card and looked at her name again and then set it on my nightstand. Why had I experienced such strong feelings while sitting across from Tonya? Was I feeling too lonely? Was I even emotionally healthy? Maybe I was actually losing my mind while I put up a strong front of a courageous recovery.

I turned off the lamp and lay uneasily in the darkness. I looked out the big bedroom window. My glance wandered upward to the stars I could see just over the hill behind our house. Were they still watching me? Were Tamara and Griffin aware of my days and long, restless nights? I knew they were there, based on my experiences, but did they look over me now?

The magic of that morning had vanished into the dark night. I rolled on my side in bed and reached down to rub the sore end of my amputated leg. The phantom pains were sometimes unbearable—strange, electric-shock sensations of pain. Sometimes I experienced even stranger sensations as specific as an itch on my third toe, a charley horse in my calf, or even a pebble in my shoe, yet the leg wasn't even there. I wondered why the pain was so intense, specific, and real. Perhaps it was my spirit simply screaming for the missing limb? Or maybe it was the dull pain of my soul screaming out for the love it once knew but had lost?

I rolled onto my back again and took one last look at the stars out the window. I said a silent prayer for Spencer for his emotional healing as I gazed into the heavens. I hoped he was doing better than I was. We didn't really talk about the accident. He avoided it even when I got the courage to bring it up. It was just too painful for either of us, so we did our best to look forward and not live in the tragedy of the past.

My last conscious thoughts wandered to the luncheon. The name on the card and the feel of those raised letters played over in my mind. Tonya. I looked over at the card sitting in the partial darkness on the nightstand. I could still see it from the moonlight coming into the window. Gazing at it, I finally faded into rest, never sure if I was really sleeping or only quieting my mind for a while from the endless questions and emotional wounds that still existed in spite of all I knew.

chapter 4

The early morning light came in through the window. I sat up quickly to check the time and hollered up the half flight of stairs for Spencer to get up for school. He was always responsive, and I could hear him immediately jump out of bed to run into his bathroom, shower, and get ready. I was lucky that way. He was easy to get going and always took the initiative to get himself out the door. He'd been helpful like that since we'd returned home. He knew my physical condition was far from what it used to be and wanted to assist me in every way.

I grabbed my crutches to get myself into the shower. It was always a little tricky showering with only one leg. Balancing on one foot on the slick, soapy shower tile took some practice. I'd installed a firm handrail to steady myself and put a plastic chair in the shower to sit on just in case. My one good leg was getting stronger from doing so much of the work, but it was far from normal. It had been crushed as well, and though the doctors had saved it, there were still six pins and a metal plate holding the knee joint together.

After the shower, I dressed as quickly as I could but was

frustrated at the time it took. Putting my prosthetic leg on properly was not something I could do quickly. Everything was a process. Even after I got the prosthetic leg on, I still could not lift my right arm above my head due to the injuries I sustained in my shoulder. Getting my clothes on took a lot of work. I finally got myself put together and quickly reached for my cane when I noticed Tonya's business card still sitting on my nightstand. I had the overwhelming feeling I should call her. I paused on the thought for a moment and then grabbed the card and stuffed it in my pocket as I headed to the main level of the house to meet my son. The time it took me to get ready had put us behind, so we grabbed a simple breakfast of Pop Tarts as we headed out the door and drove to Spencer's school.

I pulled up to the school, dropped Spencer off, and watched as he walked slowly onto the playground, where many of the kids would play before the bell rang. Spencer was not a popular child, and many of his peers teased him. The fact that his dad was now crippled and his mother and brother had been killed didn't help matters. It gave the other kids more fodder to ostracize him and treat him differently. They could be so unkind. Part of me wanted to get out and reprimand the kids as they teased or pushed at him, but I knew in my heart that if I did, it would only make things worse.

Spencer became agitated when I spoke of the accident to anyone outside of our immediate family. He didn't want anyone to know about the crash or our loss, even though the entire community was aware of it by now. Somehow, he wanted life to just move on as if nothing had happened. He wanted to hide the crash from the world. Anytime I'd speak of it in front of him, he'd pull my sleeve and give me that look that clearly said, "Dad, don't." When I asked him why, and explained that it was healthy to talk about things, he simply disagreed and said he didn't want people to know. I think it made him feel even more awkward and different than he felt already. The last thing I wanted to do was make things worse for him, so I too pushed the past away in an effort to hide my own pain.

When I arrived at work, the morning was much like any other day. The joy of spring and the vibrant energy of the day before had come and gone like a gentle breeze. The emptiness and guilt had found its way back. I made my way across the street and up to the big freight elevator at the back of the building. I avoided climbing the three flights of stairs I once raced up to get to our offices on the third floor.

Many people had already arrived, and I went straight to my office to start on my email and to look at the day's schedule. I reached into my pocket to take out my keys and felt the business card again. I took it out with the keys and set them both on my desk. Why was I so compelled to call her? The number glared at me as I sat down. I attempted to ignore it. I reached for my keyboard and noticed my wedding band still on my left hand. Why call anyway? She'd already told me she was leaving soon to take a different job. Maybe that's why it felt safe? She was leaving. What harm would there be in simply reaching out? She had no intentions of sticking around anyway; I could be a short-term friend with no motives during the few weeks she had left in town. I began scrolling through my email. Besides, I could use some company anyway, without any attachments or expectations. I wished this voice in my head would be quiet. I stopped typing, shifted in my chair, and looked down at my shoes. The conversation in my mind did not quiet, but shifted. I just sat there looking at my shoes wondering if others could tell which one was my fake foot with my shoes on.

"Hey, we're in the War Room in three minutes!" Mike, one of my work colleagues, shouted into my office from the hallway, snapping me back to reality.

"Got it. Be right there."

I made my way to the room the others were in. I sat in the meeting feeling relief from the nagging voice in my head.

Somehow keeping busy calmed me, but total focus was difficult. Most days were like that strange feeling when you walk into a room to get something and then suddenly forget what you were looking for. Today became the same, except I knew what I was looking for. The room just didn't exist where I would ever find it.

The day began to sweep me away, and I lost myself in the chaos. My business partners were kind and understanding. They couldn't possibly grasp all I was dealing with, but they were patient, knowing that even at my best, I was not "all there" at times.

I did what I could to contribute in meaningful ways, but there were still days that I just had to close my door to be alone. I wasn't sure if work was still my passion or just a distraction from the heavier things on my heart. I used to be so committed and passionate at work. The next big idea was like an exciting safari hunt every day. I was driven and invigorated by the work I did, but now, it felt more like I was killing time. Enduring the daylight simply to finally go home and escape to sleep. Nonetheless, days did go by and turn into evenings and nights: evenings of Spencer, homework, and then nights of lying in the lonely darkness of our queen-size bed that felt more like a football field with only me in it.

This day was the same. It transformed into evening, and it was time to head home. Everything felt numb again as I finished up my work. The magic of the day before had truly vanished, like a sunset. I peeked over to check the time. Tonya's business card continued to taunt me from where I had laid it that morning. I looked at it again. Why didn't I just call? Was I going to carry the card around from work to home and back again in this continual silly game? I'm not sure if it was out of frustration or intrigue, but before I got up to leave, I picked up my office phone and began dialing. Then I hung up. What was I thinking? I paused and then picked up the phone again and dialed the entire number until it rang, but then I quickly hung up again. *This is so stupid*, I thought as I used my one good arm and one leg to lift myself from the office chair and headed for the elevator.

That night was a long one. I felt the frustration of my loneliness. I was short with Spencer getting through dinner and homework and even shorter with myself getting into bed and trying to sleep. I still had pictures of Tamara all over the house like a shrine. I knew I'd never get over what happened. I felt broken from the inside out in a way that often felt like I was just observing my brokenness without the courage to change or even do anything about it. Looking at all the pieces but never attempting to see if the edges might match up somehow. I tossed and turned and simply waited for the alarm to sound as if that would grant permission for me to get up and start the whole routine over again. I'd get Spencer off to school and drag myself into the office to face another day. At least it hurried the hours along.

I arrived at work the next morning and took a deep breath. I leaned back in my chair and looked out my office window. I knew this was no way to live, yet no one could change it but me. I looked at the business card still sitting where I left it and realized what a coward I was being. I read the name again: *Tonya Skubik*. It was time to do something, to move forward in some way. What did I have to lose? I had already lost most of what mattered to me anyway. Without hesitation I picked up the phone and dialed. It rang once, my heart started pounding; twice, I swallowed hard; three times, I felt sweat forming on my upper lip; and then a fourth ring. Finally Tonya's voice sounded on the other end, but it was just her answering machine. *This is perfect*, I thought. *I can simply leave a message and not have to speak to her. Yikes, but what to say?*

After the beep, I said, "Hello, this is Jeff. We sat together at the luncheon this week at the New Yorker. By the way, this call has nothing to do with work, it's completely personal, but please call me back when you get a few minutes."

I hung up the phone, wiped the perspiration from my face with my hands, and then dried my hands on my jeans. *Okay*, I thought. *I said it was personal, so she won't return the call thinking it's business. Knowing it's personal, she'll only call back if she has any interest. Right? It's in her court.*

I was talking to myself again. Why? That's when I realized what had happened, what I had done. Did I actually make a phone call with the intention of asking this woman out? That felt strange. I thought of Tamara. What was I doing? Although she'd been gone over a year, calling another woman still felt so foreign to me. I dove into my work and went on with the day. Before too long, however, Tonya actually called back, which caught me off guard. I didn't expect to hear back from her so quickly. Now I really was going to be forced to have the conversation rather than just fantasizing about how it might go.

"Hi, Tonya. Yes, it was fun. Thanks for calling back. Listen, you mentioned you'd found it difficult to meet people here and were leaving town. I get all that, but I was wondering . . . I mean if you just want a friend or someone to hang out with, we could have dinner or something? I mean, I'm safe enough, and you're leaving anyway. I just thought, maybe, well, that we might at least enjoy each other's company. That's all. Would you join me Friday for dinner?"

I sat there, my heart pounding. I sounded so silly.

"Sure," she replied. "Where are we going? What shall I wear?"

I hadn't even gotten that far yet. "Pants or trousers will be fine," I replied. *What? Trousers. Listen to me. What am I even doing?*

"Okay. I'll just meet you at your office after work. I can be there by six."

"Perfect," I said and hung up the phone.

What was that? I couldn't believe what I had just done. It felt strange yet exciting, but it was mixed with tinges of guilt. I almost wanted to call back and say, "Never mind. I was just kidding. I just wanted to see if I would really do it." But I knew I couldn't turn back now. I had taken what was a huge step for me, and the biggest miracle in all of it was that I actually picked up the phone to make the call. I was stunned and grateful, but scared.

chapter 5

I *woke up early Friday morning and took time to* vacuum and clean up my truck. I arranged for the nanny to take Spencer to my mom's after school so I'd be free for dinner. The workday raced by, and soon it was time for my date. *Date?* I thought. *Am I crazy?* I watched out the window to see if Tonya would pull up, but then I decided to go down to the parking lot to avoid having to use the big freight elevator in front of her. I was still a bit awkward on my leg and struggled to pull down the big metal doors with my shoulder in such a tender state. I left the building and limped toward my truck. I was ten yards from it when she pulled up in her car. I went numb.

"Hello," I heard myself say as she rolled down her window. I made my way around the truck to open the door for her while she parked and walked toward me. She got out of her car in one easy motion. She was strong and athletic but with a natural flow about the way she moved. She wore dark pants with heels and a simple white button-up shirt and blazer on top. I didn't want to stare, but couldn't help notice every detail about her. She exhibited the same grace as she jumped up into the passenger seat of my truck. I closed the door and limped to the driver's side and did my best to get in effortlessly too. I was worried at first. I was so self-conscious. I kept wondering what she was thinking, and then I worried again why it mattered. It didn't take long, however, until we were engaged in meaningful conversation as we drove up the canyon to a restaurant I loved. It was lovely and quiet. Our table was near the fireplace with a view out of a large picture window, looking into the trees.

"The pepper steak here is awesome—if you feel like having steak twice in one week," I offered as we settled in.

"Sounds good to me," she said.

"I'll ask the waiter to bring you some ketchup."

I smiled. She giggled, shrugged, and said, "I dare you."

She sat back in her chair to take off her jacket. Her blazer was purple. I noticed how she gracefully slipped it off and hung it on the chair behind her. I would have offered to assist her, but by the time I even thought it, the jacket was behind her and she was leaning back onto the table, resting her elbows on it with her chin sitting on her hands. She was beautiful. Her hair had a natural part in it and was pinned back with a small dragonfly hairpin. I noticed how tastefully she had applied conservative makeup simply to highlight her eyes and lips. Somehow the way she leaned onto the table, giving me her undivided attention, and the fact that she was already comfortable enough to slip off her jacket put me so much at ease.

We ordered, and, yes, I even asked for a side of ketchup, which got a strange look from the waiter, but he brought it all the same. The conversation continued easy and unforced. She asked all the questions about the accident and what had happened. She asked about Spencer and how he was coping. I was able to maintain my composure and carry on an intelligent conversation, which actually surprised me, given I had held so much in for so long.

I kept having the strangest pings of emotions again as we sat talking. I'd feel the butterflies in my stomach but stabilizing warmth at the same time. I was able to open up as if I already knew her well. She was a good listener. I poured out many of my feelings about what had happened and what I had experienced. She had no judgment of any of it. She just listened. I shared personal insights and things I had learned over the past year. I got a little emotional talking about the car crash but was even able to share some of that with her without hesitation. We eventually lightened the subjects and even laughed a little together about work and current events. Even with the steady conversation, I still felt awkward at times. I felt as if I were doing something wrong. I kept looking over my shoulder. I hadn't dated really at all, and it felt like I was stepping out on my wife or something. Even though Tamara had passed, I always considered myself a married man—until now.

As the night rolled on, I kept having the strongest feelings of love—yes, love—come over me. Not like a romantic love, but a spiritual, unconditional love.

I had experienced something similar shortly after the accident happened. With all the life-threatening injuries I sustained, my spirit actually left my body for a while and I had found myself wandering around the hospital. As I did, I had seen into people's souls, really feeling them and knowing them to the core. Now here I was, experiencing the same thing with this beautiful woman as we ate dinner and talked.

I began to feel like I must be going crazy again. None of these emotions made sense. Why such deep, strong feelings for a stranger? I paused as it rushed over me. It began to frighten me, actually. I resolved that I must see a counselor or psychiatrist soon. How could I be feeling this, these strong rushes of love on the first date? *I know I'm losing it*, I decided as we finished our entrees and ordered dessert.

As the night continued, I was startled at how comfortable I became. We talked about many things in depth. We discussed religion and the role it had played in our lives. Tonya was a Catholic girl from Minnesota but had spent half of her time growing up in the Bible belt of Oklahoma. I was a Mormon from a dairy farm in a small town in the Utah mountains. We talked about our immediate and extended families and the backgrounds we came from. Tonya also came from dairy farmer stock in northern Minnesota, something we had in common. She was the oldest of three in her family and was quite close to her siblings, especially her younger sister, Tricia. We even talked about football and what was going on the in NFL that season. Mostly, we talked about spiritual things. I opened up enough to share some of the profound out-of-body experiences I had after the accident and during my time in the hospital. I was actually enjoying myself and enjoying Tonya's company. It felt good to share so openly with someone outside of my immediate family and close work friends. The only uncomfortable aspect of the situation was, oddly enough, my comfort. My mind didn't know how to take it. I felt bad that I felt good, and yet I didn't want it to end.

By the time I dropped Tonya off and headed for home, it was way too late to pick up Spencer. I would call my mom and ask if he could just spend the night with her and I would pick him up in the morning. As I reached over to grab my cell phone I realized I was still wearing the wedding band Tamara had given me. What was I doing? Had Tonya noticed? That smothering, doubtful feeling started setting in again. My mom picked up the call.

"Hi mom. Sorry it's so late. I'm glad you're still up though. Is Spencer doing ok?"

"He's already sound asleep, and it's perfectly fine," my mom replied. "How did things go?"

I didn't know what to say, and I didn't want to talk about it. I was confused by what I was feeling, the joy and excitement of the experience with a heavy dose of guilt and questions about what I was even doing. "Fine," I said and changed the subject. "I'll see you in the morning, Ma. Let Spencer sleep in, and I'll be by around ten."

Sitting in the silence of the ride home, I became a bundle of nerves and emotions. What had I done? Why did I feel the way I did? By the time I got home I was a wreck. My eyes were wet with tears over the grief of losing my wife and youngest son. My heart became heavy with the guilt that I was driving the car the day of the crash. It was my fault, I felt. And now this—I'm out gallivanting with strange women and feeling all kinds of love-like emotions. I couldn't decide whether that was bad or good.

When I got home I made my way up the stairs and collapsed on my bed in a heap of private tears. "Help me, God," I uttered out between sobs. "I don't know what's wrong with me, but I'm sure I'm losing my mind. I went out to dinner with a woman," I blurted out, as if God didn't know already. "And I enjoyed it, but I'm losing it. I'm really going crazy because I kept feeling love—like real love—for her, and I don't even know her. Help me, Father. I'm afraid I need a shrink. I think I might be going crazy or something. I miss Tamara so badly, and it hurts so deep, yet tonight I felt happy. I felt love all around me. I . . ."

I rolled onto my back and took a deep breath. I felt the hot tears roll from the corners of my eyes and down into my ears. Then I heard it, not in my head, but in the core of my soul. I heard that still, small voice that speaks to the heart, and it said in a plain and powerful way, "The love you're feeling is not *your* love; it's my love for her."

I lay there on my back catching my breath. I wiped the tears from off the sides of my face. *His love for her? Wow. Maybe that's why it feels so wonderful.*

I took a deep breath. I was actually exhausted. I quickly got undressed, took off my prosthetic leg, switched off the light, and faded off to sleep.

chapter 6

I *awoke with a start. It was strange to wake* up to an empty house. *Spencer!* I thought. *My son.* I needed to check on him, so I quickly sat up, stood, and—steadying myself on the bed—picked up my phone to call my mom. The display read 6:32 a.m. They wouldn't even be up yet. I sat back down and rubbed my eyes. Why was I so jittery? I replayed the events of the night before. They all felt a bit like a dream as I grabbed my crutches and made my way to the shower. Trying to go back to sleep was useless. I continued to replay the events of the previous night as the hot water raced over my body. How Tonya looked, what she said, how nice it was to share conversation like that. I got out of the shower and grabbed a pair of comfortable jeans and my favorite pearl-snap button shirt. As I dressed and prepared to put the leg back on, I realized this new routine was never going away. No matter what I felt the night before—love, comfort—this routine of putting on the leg would always be painful and might cause bitter reflections. *I'll never forget,* I thought as I pulled my stump into the cold, hard socket. *This process is so I'll always remember what I had and what I lost.* Guilt plagued me again as I recounted the events of the previous night. *What am I doing?* I secured the leg on tight with the suction valve, pulled up my jeans, and took the phone from my pocket—7:22 a.m. I still had over two hours before I had to pick up my son, but there was something I knew I wanted to do first.

The sun was in full view over the eastern hills as I drove down Bountiful Boulevard to the cemetery where Tamara and Griffin were buried. My thoughts rushed to my grief again, and I fought back tears while I parked the truck, grabbed my cane, and made my way down the grassy hill to their markers. They had been buried on the south end of the cemetery near a lovely little evergreen tree. I stayed focused on the tree as I made my climb down the hill. Uneven terrain was the most difficult to navigate with the prosthetic leg. By the time I arrived, the tears could be dammed no longer. They rushed freely down my face as I collapsed on the grave of my deceased wife and son. We had buried them together in the same casket. I knew she'd want it that way. My body heaved as I poured out my soul into the cold wet grass underneath me. "I don't know what I'm doing, Tam. I went on a date last night with a woman named Tonya. I'm sorry. I don't know what I'm doing. I miss you. I miss you so badly! I love you. Please come back to me. Please come back somehow. I can't do this anymore."

I banged my head on the grass and wiped my eyes. I realized what I must've looked like, although no one was around to see me. I envisioned myself, a crippled man prostrate on the ground, sobbing over the grave of his loved ones. I knew I was creating quite a scene even if no one could see it. I collected my composure long enough to sit up and look at the grave markers. Tamara and Griffin were gone. They were really gone. The names and dates stared back at me with the same metallic coldness they were engraved in. I wiped my eyes and found my way to my knees. Getting up was always awkward with one leg. I looked up at the sun, now gleaming down from behind light, wispy clouds. What was I going to do? How could I ever survive this? I could never love again, at least not like I had. But, at only thirty-five, the thought of remaining single the rest of my life seemed quite bleak.

I struggled to my feet and hobbled back to the truck. I made my way down the small residential streets of the foothills and onto the interstate, heading south toward my mom's house. I didn't play the radio. I just drove, deep in thought. What had happened last night? Was I being selfish? Was I motivated only by loneliness? Why all the feelings? And why did I feel so guilty about it? Yet even in the guilt and confusion, I wanted to see Tonya again. None of it made sense. We had so little in common. I was a Mormon from Utah, and she was a Catholic from Minnesota who would soon be leaving town anyway.

When I arrived at my mom's, she was putting the customary big breakfast on the table: bacon, eggs, pancakes, and orange juice. Spencer was up and had been watching cartoons in the living room while Grandma cooked. I hurried in to him and gave him a big hug. The tears almost returned as I held him and wondered if I was betraying him too somehow. His cheerful mood kept my feelings in check and assured me he was fine. He loved sleeping over at Grandma's and seemed unconcerned about my absence at all. We all ate together and only discussed the drawings my mom and Spencer had done together and the card games they had played. My mom must have sensed my unwillingness to talk about the events of the night before and held her questions for a more private time.

I was afraid to speak about my date and still felt kind of guilty for going. Yet not an hour passed that I didn't think about how good it felt to be with someone and have meaningful conversation. But what of the strange, strong love I had felt sitting across the table at dinner and the whisper that had come to me when I asked God why? I wanted to call Tonya again. I wanted to reach out and feel that love all over again. I wanted to laugh. I wanted to watch her put ketchup on her steak, but I was still concerned that I was now a puppet in this crazy self-created illusion of mine.

chapter 7

I was lost in my thoughts throughout the next day. Spencer and I went through our regular Sunday routine. We slept in a little later and had breakfast together at the small kitchen nook table. I played music on the stereo loud enough to fill the house with beautiful tones. He was happy and had no idea what emotions I was experiencing. He hadn't even asked where I'd been two nights ago. I didn't tell him. I was so torn about how much to share with him. He was just a little boy. He had experienced enough hurt and confusion in his life already. My job as his dad was to provide some stability, something he could count on. I wondered what that might look like in the future. Was I really protecting him by keeping it just the two of us? Would a woman in our lives just complicate things more? I knew I could never replace his mom, but he deserved a mother's love. And I deserved a woman's love as well.

After breakfast we got dressed in Sunday jackets and ties and made our way to our chapel, which was just down the street. I didn't even speak to anyone in our congregation when we got there. I was stuck somewhere between feeling selfish and totally intrigued with what I had experienced on my date with Tonya. I wondered what people would think. Would family and friends feel it was too soon for a relationship, that I should give things more time, or would they be glad I was taking steps toward moving forward? My mind was an endless blog of what-ifs that really didn't even matter at this point. So what? I went on a date and felt something. At least I could feel. Yes, it was causing all kinds of ping-pong feelings, but at least I knew I was alive.

Monday came and the workweek rolled in. Spencer and I returned to our regular schedule of school, homework, and the nanny taking care of things until I got home. The urge to call Tonya continued, and I easily gave into it. Back at work that Monday, it wasn't even lunchtime before I called her and arranged to meet that night—for a few minutes—after I finished at the office. With Spencer at home I got creative about how to ease him and Tonya into things. I didn't feel comfortable springing her on him, or him on her for that matter. I wasn't sure about how far to take things with Tonya leaving. I was sensitive to Spencer's emotions as well. Nonetheless, Tonya and I met almost daily after that. We would make plans for lunch or play a quick game of pool in the pub below my office after work. Mostly we just talked—usually long late-night phone conversations after Spencer had gone to bed. I would introduce her to him in time, when it made sense. I just wasn't sure how to do so, and whether the timing would ever be right. What would I say? "This is the woman I'm eating dinner with sometimes and talking to on the phone"? Or "Meet my new girlfriend; she's leaving in a month so we're just having fun"? None of it made sense. And I was still far from being over my grief of losing Tamara and Griffin. All I knew was that I appreciated the company and wasn't willing to let it go.

I worried at times that I might be simply filling the big void within myself. I didn't want to play games with anyone, especially my son Spencer, but I felt compelled to keep going, to see it play out. I knew Tonya would be leaving soon for Arizona and flirted with the notion that everything would simply come to an abrupt halt after she left. The thought hurt. The love I had felt for her from the first date continued to grow. I was developing my own feelings independent of what I'd been told was "God's love for her." Romantic urges were surfacing as well, which I had no idea what to do with. I struggled with all I was feeling. At times I felt selfish, at others like this was the perfect thing for Spencer and me, but in the end I knew I was falling in love, too hard and too fast, but I was falling, and somewhere in the free fall I felt joy. Healing was in Tonya's touch, in her voice, in her laughter. Her energy filled me with excitement, but with a quiet comfort as well. I enjoyed being with her, even with all the mixed emotions it brought up. In the process I had actually decided to remove the wedding band my late wife Tamara had given me. I was indeed single, even if I still grieved the loss of my first marriage. The night I took it off was a painful one. It was like losing another part of me in many ways. I kept it in a small box in my nightstand with other things I counted as sacred. I knew the ring was just a symbol, and taking it off was a symbol too. It was a symbol of being open to other possibilities. Being open to what doors might open since the ones I had adored for so long were now shut.

I eventually invited Tonya to our house. I wasn't sure what to do, however. I still had photos of Tamara and our family in almost every room. Should I take them all down? Or would that only be fooling Tonya—and myself—that I was truly moving forward when I was really still grappling with many of my feelings? I wondered if I was only leaning into my relationship with Tonya knowing she was leaving soon. Was it just a false deadline with nothing beyond that? Everything was becoming complicated. I wasn't sure whether Tonya was a mask to my pain or my deliverance from it. Was I only searching for what I'd lost? Or was the true answer to joy right there before me? I didn't know, but I wanted to keep letting her in. I wanted her even closer. In my deepest heart, I didn't want her to leave so soon. I wanted time, time to see what played out and how I felt over time, but I wasn't sure how to ask for that. I knew, however, that I could only take one step at a time, the first being to invite her to our house and eventually introduce her to Spencer.

I decided to leave the photos up. I had nothing to hide. Many of our conversations had already revolved around the accident and my loss, but I hadn't revealed to Tonya all that I was going through emotionally with my newfound feelings for her. I felt she also wanted to meet Spencer, but I didn't want to confuse him by bringing a woman into our picture yet. Why introduce him to Tonya when I knew she was leaving anyway? It felt better to keep my relationship with Tonya from him for now. I didn't want to tear his emotional wounds open or cause him to think I was moving forward and leaving him behind in some way. I arranged for him to visit his cousins the night Tonya came over, to simplify things.

Tonya came to the house. I had cleaned it well, but I left everything just as it had been. Tonya noticed all the photos of my late wife, my late son, and the entire family as soon as she came through the front door. It must have been quite weird for her. I had frames highlighting memories of a ten-year marriage in almost every room.

I had too much respect for Tamara to remove the photographs for a woman that was leaving town in two weeks. Yet in some strange way, I felt like I was actually introducing Tonya to the entire family through the photos. It was a bit psychotic, I know, but it seemed almost natural given the state I was in.

Tonya looked at many pictures of Spencer, and the conversation quickly turned to him.

"Do I get to meet him?" Tonya asked.

"Soon," I replied.

The question threw me, so I guided Tonya to the kitchen, where we could escape the gaze of the photos for a while. I didn't want to tell Tonya that my intention was to wait until things got serious before I introduced her to Spencer. I was worried about what Spencer would think about bringing another woman into our home as well. Would he think I was replacing his mother? I also didn't want Tonya to feel pressured since she would be leaving town anyway. I purposely left all the other doors to rooms in the house closed. I knew if Tonya caught a glimpse of Tamara's sweater still lying over the chair next to my bed, she would really know how shattered I was. A rush of uncertainty about everything I was doing came over me again. I had such a hole in my heart to fill, and I knew no one could ever fill it. Still, I just wanted to be normal again. I wanted to feel like a whole man, and, somehow, Tonya had brought a taste of that. Her intense interest in me along with her acceptance of my brokenness brought me peace and courage. That felt good to me.

chapter 8

All of the emotions swirling around in the whirlwind of my and Tonya's relationship had become overwhelming to me. She was leaving, and I didn't want her to go. I wanted her to meet my son, but I didn't want to complicate things. Time and good judgment had lost all relevance. I was already in way too deep, even in the short few weeks we had spent together. I loved Tonya. I had from the first time I saw her dipping her steak into ketchup. I would have never even called her had I not been overrun with such promptings from the beginning. And the more time we spent together, the deeper the feelings grew. It felt natural but foreign to me. We'd drawn clear lines about the physicality of our relationship, so why was I ashamed? I had been widowed for well over a year. I realized how starved I was for affection. Yet I also realized that over those many months, I felt as if I were still married. I had never let go of Tamara. But Tonya's affection unlocked something that I had been keeping in chains for so long, the human part of me that was a lonely man.

Guilt would only crash against the waves of what felt magical to me. But how could I be in love and grieving for the wife of my youth yet craving the woman in my arms? The polarity of my feelings confused me. My heart was expanding and dividing between the wife I loved and lost and the woman who had so miraculously appeared in my life.

Overwhelmed with conflicting feelings, I headed to my place of comfort. Once again, I found myself in the cemetery on Tamara's grave, sobbing in a heap. It was early morning again, so no one was around, but I didn't care who saw me this time. It was time to finally let go and address all that was on my heart. I wondered if Tamara could hear me. Was I praying to her or for her? I wasn't sure, but the purity of my emotions came flowing through the sobs:

"I'm having feelings for another woman, Tam. I don't know what to do. Please forgive me. I can't live without you, but I don't know how I'm going to do this. I feel so ashamed yet happy at the same time. Please help me. Please guide me. I'm so worried about Spencer . . ."

My deepest desires wept out onto the cool grass around the graves. I didn't hold back the tears and grieved openly in honest confession about everything I was experiencing. I blurted out how much I still missed her. How much I missed them. How much I loved them and yet how my heart was expanding in painful and wonderful ways.

I was there for some time, gasping out my deepest fears and desires. I could barely see through my swollen eyes when I sat up and looked at the markers again. I looked at the names, the dates, and rubbed my fingers over the raised, bronze letters on the headstone. All the pain of what had happened rushed over me. They were gone. And I would never be the same.

"Tam," I whispered under my breath, "I really need you." But the stillness in the air reminded me of just how alone I was, there in the cemetery. I felt another hot tear well up and roll over my lower eyelid. It fell on the headstone right by Tamara's name. As I watched it dry in the sun, I felt a numbness start at the top of my head and travel down to the base of my spine. Warmth began to engulf my entire body. My entire frame felt like it was vibrating, and everything around me became crystal clear. Heat began to radiate into my shoulders and neck. A familiar energy settled right between my shoulder blades, and that's when I felt it. It was her. I knew Tamara was there with me. I felt her love and spirit as real as if she had walked up behind me. As I sat looking over her name on the headstone, I could feel her in my heart and right there with me. I felt her actually standing with her hands on my shoulders as I sat and wept. I turned toward her and saw nothing, and I reached out to touch her and felt nothing, yet I knew she was there. I could never forget her touch and the feeling Tamara brought with her wherever she was.

I struggled to my feet and felt as if she actually embraced me. The feelings were so real it was undeniable. I felt her arms around my neck and her body close to mine even though I could not see her. It was as real as anything I had ever experienced. Pure intelligence rushed into my heart. Her voice spoke to me in the same tones it had when she was alive—those loving, knowing tones.

"My Jeff, you silly goose. Do you not know you can choose whomever you want? My deepest desire is for you to be happy. I don't want you to be alone. You are free to do whatever you wish. Your joy is my joy, and your pain is my pain. We are linked even in death, but please know this: I have sent Tonya to you. That's why you've had all the feelings you've been experiencing. The first time you saw her, all the déjà vu, even your romantic urges. They were all messages from me. Don't you see? I can do that from here. I'm still connected to you, and it is not only my right, but my privilege. It's different here. There is only wisdom. Only love. No jealousy, judgment, or possession. I want you to learn this too. That's the reason I have sent Tonya to you. She will teach you unconditional love. And that—in spite of all you've been through and learned—is the one thing you still get to work on. Unconditional love. It's all about love."

As I felt her words, my surroundings seemed to disappear and I stood in a magical realm of light. I saw a vivid picture of a small pebble hitting a smooth surface of water, as if it were right in front of me. The ripples fanned out from it in eternal waves, never ending.

"Do you see what you have the opportunity to create here?" Tamara whispered to me. Then she repeated the same phrase I had heard right after our accident when my own spirit had left my body for that brief moment in time, "To what degree have you learned to love?"

I stood there, feeling the sun on my face as I let the tears fall freely onto my chest.

"Stay with me, Tam. I want you here."

"Choose joy," she reminded me, as I had been told before.

I felt her leaving.

"Don't go. Please!"

But the reality of her fading away reinforced the fact that she had literally been with me.

I had an answer. The words "Choose joy" echoed in my heart. Those words I had been given during one of the darkest nights of my soul when I wondered how I would ever make it. When I cried to God and asked why—why had all this happened and how would I ever make it? "Choose joy" was the answer then, and again now. I knew my next step, even if none of it made sense.

I resolved to love Tonya without any shame or guilt. She was what I wanted. I had received so many spiritual insights now. I knew she had been sent—that she was a gift from above. The bottom line was quite plain: I had fallen in love with her. It was that simple. It didn't need to be any more complicated than that. Love—that was reason enough to let down my walls and finally begin to choose joy.

chapter 9

I'*m leaving next week for Tempe,*" Tonya said without hesitation as we talked on the phone. I had a break in my workday and decided to call her. She continued, "My sister will meet me there in a month or so. I want to find an apartment and get all set up before she comes. I've already accepted my new job. I just have to figure out how to get all my stuff moved down there. I think I'll hire a moving company to haul it for me once I know where I'll be."

It hit me like a brisk crosswind. The time had passed so quickly. "Wow, it's here already isn't it?"

"Yes, I can't see you this weekend. I'm loading the bare necessities into my car and heading out Friday. My last day on the job here in Salt Lake is Wednesday."

"Do you have time for lunch on Wednesday? I'd like to see you before you go."

"Of course. I'll make time."

I hung up the phone and looked at the clock on my office wall. Maybe I had been wrong about all this. But I was sure it wasn't just my imagination at the gravesite. Tamara had spoken to me, and everything I had experienced up to this point was pointing to Tonya. She had magically shown up in my life, and now she was leaving just as quickly as she had appeared.

I hurried through my work and headed home. My mom was watching Spencer that day because the nanny had taken a long weekend trip with friends. When I arrived home, my mom had done the laundry and was just folding the last batch of whites to put in my dresser. I could smell dinner in the oven, and Spencer was happily painting pictures at the kitchen table. Thank goodness for moms.

We ate together, cleaned up, and then talked and laughed while we worked on one of those silly three-dimensional puzzles of a human face Spencer had gotten as a birthday gift months before.

There was such peace in the house. I adored my mother for all she did. She had been so supportive through the entire ordeal. After Spencer had gone to bed, my mom lingered to talk as she slowly and methodically put the dishes into the dishwasher, and, as moms often do, she asked all the questions about Tonya and what was happening in my life.

I answered with short vague answers until I realized she had finished loading the dishwasher as slowly as she possibly could without me really telling her anything. I finally opened up as she picked up her purse to leave. I realized I didn't want her to go without sharing with her how I was feeling. We sat back down at the kitchen table as I told her what was happening to me: how Tonya was leaving—moving to Arizona—and how I wasn't sure what to do about it. I didn't want to come off as a needy weirdo, I explained. But what could I say in this situation but good-bye and good luck? I paused. "I don't know why I want this so bad, Mom, but I do."

My mom's face looked sober and empathetic, but her eyes seemed to smile as if she were happy that her son was actually feeling again. She got up from the table, hugged me, and simply reminded me that I had all my own answers as she grabbed her things and headed for her car.

I watched from the window while she drove away. I turned and headed up the stairs, using the handrail to do most of the upward pulling with my arms. Halfway up, I glanced back down at the spotless kitchen and listened to the dishwasher as it ran. It was nice to have my mom there.

A woman's touch was absent in our home. I missed the way Tamara had always held the house together. I felt I was a good dad but, honestly, a pretty lousy mom. My heart ached for Spencer. Would he ever remember what it used to be like before the wreck, when his own mother was there? Would he ever forgive me for the trauma the accident had put him through?

I pulled myself the rest the way up the stairs and made my way to the bed to take off my prosthetic leg. Would I ever feel whole again? Was I simply flattered that a beautiful young woman had actually taken interest in me? And had she, really? Or was this all an illusion in my own mind? She was leaving. Maybe the magic I had been experiencing was just my one-way wild imagination?

The quiet of the loneliness closed in on me as I lay on the bed and shut my eyes. *Should I call Tonya and tell her not to leave? Should I ask her to stay here with us and see what we might create together?* Maybe I was just holding her captive in my pain when she had a whole life to move on to. She could be free to find her own joy outside of my pain.

In spite of the amazing experience I'd had, my heart was still filled with doubt. I said a silent prayer, "Guide me, Lord. Don't let my imagination or my heart run away with me. Allow me the wisdom to do the best thing." But what was that? I knew how I felt and what I had experienced, but what if Tonya didn't feel the same? She had never once brought up an alternative to leaving for Arizona to meet her sister and start fresh there. I also knew I was still grieving. I was so broken in many ways that it frightened me. I didn't want to tell Tonya. If she knew all the doubt mixed with love I was experiencing, I feared it would only complicate things even further. And if she knew how broken that made me feel, could she ever really love me?

I finally slipped into a light, restless slumber with that burning question still on my mind: Did she love me? The question was coupled with the worry of what was next and what was best for my son. The confusion was as smothering as the thick, bulky comforter on the bed. I stirred just long enough to throw the down comforter aside and lie in the coolness of the breeze coming in from the open window. It was just enough to lull me to sleep.

chapter 10

I *awoke with the resolve that I would not just* let Tonya go—not without at least telling her how I felt. The stirrings were deep, and she deserved to know my heart even if my feelings were only one-sided.

We met for lunch. The situation already seemed strange. I didn't know how to approach the subject, so I just blurted it out over the awkward small talk of her moving plans.

"What if you didn't go? What if you just stayed here and we saw how things might play out between us? The truth is, I don't want you to go. I want you to stay here and see how our relationship might play out."

She paused; the silence was too long, but then she giggled nervously a little and moved onto more small talk of when the moving company would be coming to pick up her furniture and if I could assist them with collecting it when they came.

I wanted to shout, "Stop! No, you're not listening to me." I wanted to tell her that this had been plaguing me for weeks and that I had actually broken down on my deceased wife's grave just days ago about my feelings for her and that I had an undeniable experience—but I didn't. I still feared she would see me as some deranged man living in a fantasy of how I would put my life back together. Her body language and nervous response also gave me the clear signal that she wasn't interested in a conversation like that. So I sat in silence just listening to her, feeling my head nod in the affirmative that I would assist her with the moving company once she arrived in Arizona.

I felt like an idiot. Why did I even ask? It was obviously too soon. In reality, she barely knew me. And why did I feel I had to force the issue anyway? Why couldn't I simply trust that angels were at work in my behalf and let things play out as they were intended to?

I sat there blushing and feeling silly as I sipped my water and avoided eye contact with Tonya. I didn't want my food. I felt like a politician simply agreeing and saying what I wanted her to hear. I watched myself commit to everything she was saying about getting out of town. I was ignoring all of my own feelings. Was this my only chance? No other woman would show interest in a one-legged man with a son. And I wanted her—not only because of the experience I had at the gravesite, but because I was falling in love with her. But she was resolved to leave.

Tonya finished her lunch; mine sat untouched on the plate since my question. We got up to leave, and I resolved that she was walking out of my life. What did I expect really? None of this made sense, and the spiritual things I had been experiencing would never jive with the ego and natural progression of things.

Tonya left at the end of the week as planned. We had a long phone conversation as she drove. I pretended that I just wanted to make sure she arrived safely, but deep down it was my way of holding on for a little longer. The conversations continued nightly, but they were filled only with the details of her search for a new apartment, her new job, and the typical daily activities.

It took me by surprise when she announced that she would be coming back to Salt Lake for the weekend to tie up some loose ends here. I jumped at the opportunity and made plans immediately for her to spend time with us and meet Spencer. It was nice because it actually felt as if the pressure was off, somehow, with her having left town. It had also given me a chance to look at things with a different perspective while she was away for that first two weeks. I had been so determined to make the relationship work out that I had forgotten to simply trust the fact that the spiritual answers had already come. I had made a new commitment to let things be. Whatever was meant to turn out would, and there was no need for me to push or force things. I was more relaxed about the relationship and had decided now to be okay with whatever happened.

It felt so much better. In fact, the message I had received at the gravesite—to learn unconditional love—made more sense now with this new perspective. I could love Tonya without stipulations of what our relationship should become or what it should look like. That changed my entire demeanor about us into something much more natural and easy.

Tonya arrived on Friday evening and spent her entire Saturday with us. Her visit was delightful. Her meeting Spencer went wonderfully, and they got along splendidly. Spencer was excited to meet her. He took her for a short hike on the back hill behind our house after lunch to gather wildflowers. I watched as they made their way down the small game trail and through the oak and wild maples. I hadn't realized how he must have missed having someone to hike with. The back hill was far too steep for me to manage with my leg now, and we hadn't been out on the hill since the accident had happened. He was giddy, pointing things out to her and being quite talkative. She laughed and conversed with him in a way that was beautiful. It was hardly fair to my heart to see them together like that. As they walked down on the lower trail, I saw Spencer reach over to take her hand, not to hold it really, but simply to pull her in another direction toward the south end of the lot where the larger maple trees grew.

But when I saw him reach out to grab her hand, I experienced even deeper love for Tonya. In fact, she looked so much like Tamara in that moment as she walked with Spencer it almost startled me. It was the way her hair bounced as she laughed and how they interacted. Spencer was warm and uninhibited toward her. Tonya was comfortable which caused my soul to smile. I watched from the deck and reminded myself to be cool and trust the process without putting any expectations on her or anything else. I simply watched and delighted in their happiness.

That night, we all played Yahtzee at the kitchen table and laughed together until our stomachs hurt. What was meant to be just one game turned into a best-of-three tournament that went well into the night. I don't even remember who won, and it didn't matter. We laughed and had fun. There was no pressure about anything. Later, after Spencer had actually gone to bed, Tonya explained that the relationship would really never work. She was now settling in Arizona, and she didn't want to give the wrong impression by being there. As odd as it was, it came as no surprise to me. I was calm and actually content. I smiled and simply rubbed her shoulder.

"I know," I said calmly. "And thank you for today. It meant a lot to both of us."

She hugged me. I held her tight. I really was okay with letting her go even though the day had been so awesome. That was so liberating. I didn't have to make something happen or devise a plan of action toward some desired ending. For all I knew, this was the end of our relationship. And I was at peace with it. I had no expectations and no desired outcome, simply that moment—the gratitude for having that peace in the present moment.

"Do me a favor," I whispered as I held her. "Don't forget how this feels, okay. No matter where life takes you and what you experience, remember how this feels."

She kissed me and said, "I will. I promise."

Saturday became Sunday, and I knew Tonya would be leaving

again that day. She actually ended up coming to church with us. She had always wondered what a Mormon service must look like and decided to join us probably more out of curiosity than anything. It was like we just wanted to bask in the peace of the day before. Odd, but knowing it was over was almost magnetically driving us closer. Even if we were just friends, it was another hour we could spend together before she flew away again. Even that time was calm and happy, and it was nice to have someone sit by me. She even sang the hymns, and I enjoyed listening to her voice. We drove her to the airport that evening, and Spencer chattered continually about the animal facts book he brought along. He told her all along the way about everything from how far whales migrate and the territory one mountain lion can cover to how much a chipmunk can carry in its mouth. Tonya listened patiently and laughed with Spencer until it was time to send her to the departure gate. We shared one last big hug and she was off.

We still exchanged emails and talked over the phone on a daily basis. We couldn't seem to stay away. I had lots of frequent flyer miles saved up, and we often made silly wagers on the Yahtzee games we'd play at the table, Spencer included, which led to additional visits to Salt Lake. Every weekend visit seemed to end with a Saturday night Yahtzee game, the loser providing a ticket to the winner. I'd lose on purpose.

Our relationship continued to progress, and even though we had decided it would never work out, it seemed to be working out wonderfully. Months passed, all the while with Tonya visiting us in Salt Lake or me visiting her in Arizona, but we stayed connected. The long distance relationship added depth in a way that allowed us to connect on deeper levels. Without the physical proximity, we connected soul to soul, which was far more powerful than mere physical attraction. The relationship had naturally developed into something quite beautiful, and it happened naturally without force or expectations. It was actually in an email that Tonya eventually asked, "Where is all this going?" What we had been so willing to let go of had developed into something neither of us wanted to be without. I knew it was in my court as to where to take next steps and to what level, but knowing Tonya was open to, maybe even hoping for, that kind of commitment, created a space where I finally felt safe going.

chapter 11

The first person I consulted was my eight-year-old son, Spencer. We had talked a lot about Tonya, and he enjoyed her visits. They had developed a relationship, but it was only so deep based on Tonya's brief weekend visits. Tonya and I had also discussed Spencer at length and what it all meant for her should we continue our courtship. The questions still had to be asked, however, and I knew this was as important to Spencer as it was to me. It's funny how simple his response was. Kids have a way of cutting to the chase and getting to clarity much quicker than we do. They speak truth.

"So, how would you feel if we had Tonya around more often, more permanently?" I asked him as we drove in the truck to go visit family.

"That would be awesome, Dad, but what do you mean?" Spencer replied.

"Well, I mean like having her move back here to Utah, you know, giving her a reason to?"

"You mean like getting married?"

He said it; I didn't.

"Yes, like getting married maybe."

"Well that's easy, Dad. You just ask God if she's the right one, and he'll let you know in some way that she is."

Wow. It really was that simple. I felt I had already been given the answer months ago, yet here we were at the actualization of such a prospect. Spencer was right, and I already had my answer. At least he was supportive and not resentful about the possibility. The only missing key was that Tonya would still have to say yes.

She would be coming to Salt Lake again that weekend. I didn't want a fancy or cliché engagement. I decided I would pop the big question in a unique and meaningful way.

It had been a bit of a whirlwind romance with airplane tickets and back-to-back weekend plans. I wanted to bring it all down to earth in a way with a simple, real proposal. I wanted to show myself at the core of who I was. Bottom line—I'm a simple farm boy, so I decided to propose back on the farm I grew up on. We had a lower pasture that ran along a small canal, which was only about a hundred yards from the upper Provo River. There was a bridge that spanned the river, and I had sat there as a boy, dangling my feet off it and contemplating my life and dreams as I watched the current run powerfully and continuously under me. I decided that I would pop the question there—on that bridge where the energy of my authentic self resided and the hopes and dreams of my youth were born.

I had a small table set up on the bridge with a nice tablecloth on it, two chairs, and one single candle in the middle. There was a dirt lane leading to the bridge that would easily accommodate my truck. I could drive right to the bridge, sit Tonya at the table, and express my feelings. It was simple, authentic, and didn't give any false pretense. It was who I was, and that's what I wanted her to see. I wanted her to see past the advertising executive, the creative director, the widower, and see me—the simple farm boy who was striving to put a life back together not only for myself but also, more important, for my son.

I purchased a ring to make it all legitimate, and I knew enough of Tonya's taste to be confident it was what she wanted. I had actually had it designed and handmade by a jeweler friend from a sketch Tonya had made over a conversation we had had weeks earlier about the perfect ring. Everything was set. The ring was ready, and the table was all set up on the bridge. I only had to pick Tonya up at the airport and ask the question.

Tonya's flight was delayed and she got in later than expected. The sun was down and it was already getting dark. The drive to the bridge was quiet. I had only told her I wanted to show her something and left it at that. As we drove, the weather became stormy. A light rain was falling by the time we drove onto the old farmstead. I pointed out my childhood home, the big weeping willow tree and the large red barn, including the rope swing we had played on as boys. As we made our way down the dirt lane, the rain worsened and was falling quite heavily by the time I reached the bridge with the table and candle on it. Oddly enough, the candle burned brightly in spite of the rain. It acted as a glowing beacon to guide our steps as we made our way to it. It was quite a sight to see the little nicely set table on the old country bridge with the rain falling all around it. I grabbed an umbrella from the back of the truck and walked Tonya toward the table. I could sense her curiosity and her anticipation. I sat her down under the umbrella, and with rain now running over my head and face, I told her how I felt and why I had chosen this humble setting to have the most important conversation of my life. The rain dripped down over my eyebrows and we laughed as I stooped from the chair and actually got down on one knee. Then I asked the question: "Are you willing to not only be my wife, but to be Spencer's mother too?"

I then presented the ring in classic fashion and waited, soaked in rain, for her response. She actually giggled a little, and her laughter soon turned into tears as she said, "Yes! Of course, yes!" She sprung from the chair and assisted me to my feet. We hugged in the rain, laughing and crying. She put on the ring and we made our way back to the truck. As we looked back at the little table in the now pouring rain, the candle still burned brightly.

"The storm can't seem to put it out." Tonya remarked.

"I know. Strange, but it burns on, no matter what."

We watched as we drove back up the dirt lane, and the candle remained glowing until we had driven far enough that we could see it no more. Only the coming years would reveal how symbolic that little candle was.

chapter 12

Spencer was the first to see the ring and congratulate us both. He seemed a little apprehensive, however, at the reality of the ring on Tonya's finger. Even though he knew I was going to ask Tonya to marry me, the ring and the talk of wedding plans would still have to settle a bit. He didn't ask many questions. He just said, "Cool," and went back out to the trampoline to jump alone. Tonya watched him from the window for a while but eventually made her way down to join him on the trampoline. I watched for a moment as they jumped together then made my way up to the bedroom to contemplate my son's emotions and how I might best manage them. I always left the bedroom window open, and I could hear Tonya and Spencer on the trampoline. Their laughter and conversation among the sound of the bouncing trampoline springs gave me some reassurance. I sat in the chair in the corner of the room, and though I could no longer see Tonya and Spencer, I could hear them jumping and talking together. I knew I had made the right choice, but I had to handle a lot of emotions. I knew my neighbors and friends were all watching, and Tonya had stepped into a big shadow cast by Tamara's memory. It is always bigger than life when someone dies. People seem to idealize the deceased in a way that becomes unrealistic. Tamara was a wonderful person and had shed her influence on so many in our community. To me, though, she was simply Tamara, a loving wife and mother who had left this world way too soon. I was doing all I could to create something peaceful for Spencer and me—to capture that happiness and love we had lost.

I knew many would think I was remarrying too soon. I was sure many others would question my choice in Tonya. The community had eulogized Tamara in such a way that no one would ever fill her shoes. It bothered me. At one point I even listed in my journal all of the little quirks and imperfections Tamara had just so I could remember the real her. The way she made endless lists of everything she wanted to accomplish day to day. Her insisting that toilet paper be hung so the end always fell down over the top of the roll and not be pulled from the bottom up, or her endless commitment to never going to bed with dirty dishes in the sink. The notion that thank-you notes should always be sent out immediately and that a phone call or simply saying thank you would not do. Calling me Jeffery when I was in trouble, being an early morning person even on Saturday, and wearing socks to bed, but that's who I had loved: the beautiful, but normal, meticulous yet down-to-earth woman with all the common, normal, little idiosyncrasies that people tend to forget when someone beloved dies.

I realized that the sound from the bouncing springs on the trampoline had ceased, but I still heard voices through the open window. I concentrated to listen.

"You know, Spence, your mom and I made a deal very long ago in a different realm," I heard Tonya say in soft tones.

I pulled my focus in even tighter to hear what was being said.

"You were such an amazing boy that God decided we could share you. You were too good to leave to just one mom. Your first mom and I agreed that she would bring you into this world and get to be your mom through your early years, and then she would go back home, and I would get to be your mom as you grew into a man."

Spencer was silent. I could not see them on the trampoline in the darkness from my window, but I could feel the energy of the conversation, and it was good.

"You never have to forget or let go of your first mom. She loved you more than anything in this world. She'll always be watching over you. You just get to have two moms. You were too special to just be given to one. Think of me as your second mom. You'll have one here taking care of you and another up above looking out for us both every step of the way. Does that make sense?"

I stood to peek out the window and saw Spencer nodding his head in the affirmative.

"C'mon. Let's see who can jump highest," Tonya exclaimed as she rose up and took his hands, and they jumped together.

My heart filled with gratitude. The freshness of this wedding proposal and acceptance had made concrete something that had simply been a notion until shortly beforehand. The reality of something, even something we want, can often fill us with doubt and concern. I was aware of all I was taking on and the challenges that might come from it. Spencer was still so young, and even though this was all expected, it may have taken him by surprise to see it come to fruition. At least Tonya had clarity in that moment. I knew it was all going to be all right. There were still lots of unanswered questions for all of us, but I knew if we kept things in perspective, it would all work out fine. The answers would surely come.

chapter 13

The following weeks and months were filled with wedding plans and organizing, which all took place long distance. Tonya was still committed to her employer in Arizona, and the wedding would take place in Minnesota, where Tonya's family lived. I did all I could from Utah as we pulled together family and friends to assist us with the plans.

Spencer fell right in line with it all and agreed to be the ring bearer for the ceremony. Our plans all came together quickly and seamlessly. The only thing that wasn't coming along was my insecurities. Our courtship had been traditional, and we had agreed to reserve intimacy until our wedding night. I was so concerned about my body. The scars, the missing limb, all of it filled me with anxiety. Tonya was such a beautiful woman, and I could hardly believe that she would choose me, but she had, and that alone gave me confidence to get over my fears of being too broken to love her madly.

The wedding was beautiful. The weather was warm for fall in Minnesota, and family and friends came from all over the country to support us and wish us well. It was an outdoor garden reception,

Spencer and Tonya dancing at the wedding

and my bishop, the leader of my congregation, flew out from Utah to perform the services. Spencer was elated to be the ring bearer and even took the first dance with Tonya.

We honeymooned in Mexico and we all moved rapidly forward into adapting to new things. Tonya did her best to transition from a single, carefree career girl to full-time wife and mother. I agreed to remodel the house, allowing Tonya to make it her own. There were a lot of moving parts, and we all did our best to make it work. The transition to marriage was not without its challenges. Two cultures were melding together, and we had to let go of a lot and embrace new things. Throughout our courtship I had slowly taken down pictures of Tamara and had put everything away long before Tonya ever moved in. That was an emotional process for me. I didn't want to feel like I was completely letting go, but I wanted to be fair to Tonya by not bringing my past into our new marriage. I experienced a true depth of her character one day when I noticed that Spencer had always kept a picture of his mom on his nightstand. As Tonya was cleaning one day, I noticed as she dusted the top of the nightstand and placed the photo back in place.

"I could ask him to put that away if it bothers you at all," I explained to her.

"You will do no such thing," Tonya replied emphatically. "That is his mother. He deserves to always have a picture of her near."

As Tonya set up house and created a beautiful home of her own, she actually set out another photo of Tamara and Griffin in the main hall of the house, where we had all kinds of personal photos from our lives displayed.

"You don't have to do that. It's okay," I commented.

"I know I don't have to. I've chosen to. I am not threatened by your past or even the love you have for your first wife. An accident happened. Had it not, I wouldn't be here with you. As I witnessed you going through all the pain and knowing how much you hurt over the loss, I saw a man who could love. Knowing you had the capacity to love at that level was half the attraction in the first place. Otherwise why would I have given in to a one-legged Mormon man with a son? I had other options, you know."

She moved close and hugged me tight and kissed me on the cheek.

"It's okay," she continued, "I want the pictures up. It's a part of you. It's a part of Spencer, and now it's a part of us." She paused, looking warmly at me, assuring me with her eyes that all was well.

The months rolled on and things began to settle in. Spencer was doing well, and we were making adjustments to make the family work. I won't pretend it was easy. Tonya had taken on a lot coming into the situation cold turkey. Managing the house and the homework was, in and of itself, a full-time job—not to mention taking care of me. I had ongoing health issues, which included everything from infections in my leg to stomach and lung setbacks from the original injuries sustained in the crash. None of it was incapacitating. I continued working, but frequent visits to the doctor and even the emergency room were a common occurrence. My body was still healing and, in many ways, so was my heart. I still had pain over the loss of my wife and child. Tonya could not heal that. In many ways it was unfair for me to expect she would. It was joyful having her in my life, but she could not heal my heart—only a lot more time and myself could do that. I would never get over what had happened, but I was working on getting to used to it.

Tonya had settled in as Spencer's caregiver in wonderful ways. She was naturally a good mother. And, though it had its challenges as well, her nurturing instinct was taking over and making a huge difference in his well-being. I could tell that Tonya could see the difference she was making. I believe she found satisfaction in it. She even began discussing the notion of having more children. This took me by surprise since we had always just spoken in the realm of Spencer. In fact, Tonya already explained that she had experienced enough serious female issues in her adult life that doctors informed her that she might not have the ability to get pregnant. I was perfectly fine with that since we already had Spencer. However, Tonya was very interested in having more children, but knowing her own medical issues, she was leaning toward adopting. She felt an intense urgency to add children to our fledgling family. I was reluctant. We were still working on our relationship, and Tonya was still bonding with Spencer. It felt too soon to me, but her feelings would not go away. She had been having strong premonitions about it, especially about adopting.

She kept having intense reoccurring dreams. In the first dream her grandmother, who had recently passed away, came to our home driving a big, black limousine. Tonya found this odd since her grandmother was a hardworking and down-to-earth person, a nurse, and the wife of a dairy farmer in northern Minnesota.

She pulled up to the curb and started to unload the limo, which was full of baby supplies: diapers, cribs, high chairs, toys, blankets—everything anyone would ever need to care for a baby. Her grandmother did not speak, but continued to unload all of the baby gear as she smiled pleasantly at Tonya.

In another dream, Tonya heard a knock at the door. As she opened it she recognized the man standing there as my deceased business partner. She had never met him but recognized him from photographs I had displayed both at home and at the office. He had been killed in an airplane accident one year before I lost Tamara and Griffin. He was young, only twenty-nine. We had been good friends and had become close through working together to start our own advertising agency. He too didn't say a word in the dream, but smiled pleasantly and handed Tonya a brown paper grocery bag, which he had folded over at the top. She unfolded the top of the bag and looked at the contents. It was baby clothes. She gasped and looked up at him, but he was gone.

In a third dream, Tonya was at the airport anxiously awaiting the arrival of an airplane. She watched, waiting for her expected passenger even though she wasn't sure who it was. She watched as the passengers came off the plane, looking closely for the friend she was anxious to meet; however, she wasn't clear on who that friend was. Suddenly, a thin blonde woman about her size rushed toward her with open arms and hands full of shopping bags. She knew immediately that it was Tamara, my deceased wife, who she also had never met but recognized from photographs. They embraced, and Tonya felt a deep kinship with her. Not a word was spoken in this dream either, but the shopping bags were handed over, and again as Tonya opened them, they were filled with wonderful items for babies.

Tonya kept telling me of her strong feelings and dreams, which she knew came from inspiration. I listened intently and wondered about all of it. I knew the power of dreams and messages but was hesitant to adopt, and so soon. In honesty, I was fearful that I might feel differently toward adopted children. Perhaps I would love them less than my natural son. The whole idea filled me with anxiety, but Tonya was persistent based on what she was experiencing.

chapter 14

One evening as I returned home from work, Tonya explained that she had made an appointment with an adoption agency and wanted me to attend with her for an orientation meeting. There was no pressure, she continued. They would simply walk us through the process and show us how it all works. There was no harm in being informed, I figured, so I agreed to attend the meeting. When we arrived, there were several couples there. All of them were desperate to adopt. In fact, some of them had waited childless for years. Tonya and I both felt a little sheepish being there since we had Spencer and had only been trying to get pregnant for a few months now. Nonetheless, we listened as they explained the adoption process. Each couple was to submit a portfolio. Many of the couples had already done so, and there were several examples for us to review there at the meeting. The portfolios were beautiful with pages of photographs, family histories, and detailed explanations of family traditions—memories and intended details of what couples wanted to create with their child should they be considered and selected as an adoptive family. The portfolios would then be shown to the potential birth mothers, and from the portfolios, the birth mothers would actually select the couple or family they desired their child to be placed with.

Again, I found it odd that we were there, but we filled out a guest log with our names and contact information and stayed for the entire meeting. We saw the heartbreak of these individuals as they shared how desperately they wanted to have children and could not. We left with the resolve that we could wait, but Tonya still had the nagging feeling that it was what we were meant to do.

Less than a week later I received a phone call from the adoption agency. They asked how interested we were in adoption. When I asked why, the man on the other end of the line began to describe the situation. He said, "We have a birth mother that arrived here this morning. She has a toddler, fourteen months old, and is pregnant with a son due this fall. She wants the brothers to stay together in the same family." The words "fourteen months old" grabbed my heart. That was the age of Griffin at the time of the accident. Also the statement about "brothers staying together" got my attention. The emotions began to flood over me as I recalled all of Tonya's impressions and her conversations over the past several weeks. Somehow I knew these were my sons coming to me. A rush of warm energy washed over me as I felt the essence of what was being explained.

"Why did you call us?" I asked.

"Well, this may or may not sound odd to you, but as an adoption agency staff, we are committed to placing these children in the correct families. Quite honestly, Mr. Olsen, we pray together as a staff each morning, and as we did so today, we were all overwhelmingly impressed upon to contact you. Of course the birth mother will make the final selection, and she already has eleven portfolios to review, but if you'd like to be considered, I suggest you get your portfolio down here immediately."

"We don't have a portfolio at this point, but I will contact Tonya and get you something as soon as possible."

I called Tonya and asked if she was sitting down.

"Yes," she answered. "Why, did they call?"

"Yes in fact they did. And they want us to get them some materials right away to be considered by a birth mother today."

"I knew it," Tonya replied. "I've been feeling it all morning. I knew something was up."

Tonya quickly hand-scrawled a letter and selected a few snapshots to put into an envelope with the letter. That would have to be our portfolio at this point. It was all we had time for and might have seemed quite quaint among all the beautiful portfolios, but something told me this was meant to be and that these boys here coming to our home.

Sure enough, we got a call from the adoption agency later that afternoon informing us that the birth mother had selected us as the family she wanted both her sons placed with. The counselor explained that as soon as she opened the letter and saw the photos, she began to tear up. Even among all the wonderful portfolios, she just had a feeling about us. And after reading Tonya's letter, she knew we were the ones. She insisted that she meet us first in person, though, just to be sure she was making the right decision, but she said her heart knew the answer.

We agreed to meet her the next day and, after a short visit, it was decided that we would meet Zach, her fourteen-month-old son, the next day at the zoo. It was a beautiful, clear day. Spencer came as well to meet the birth mother and to meet Zach. Zach was already toddling about and was big for fourteen months. When we all sat down, he actually climbed off of his birth mother's lap and went directly to Spencer. Although Zach didn't talk at this point, he laughed and gave Spencer a hug and then started doing a sort of stomping dance in front of him. When he made his way to me he actually put his hands on my face and said plainly, "Dad." I held him for a while as he patted my cheeks and played with my face, and then I handed him to Tonya. He was as comfortable in her arms as anything. He laid his head on her chest and started to stroke her wavy strawberry-blonde hair.

That pretty much sealed the deal. I felt the love and the energy of that little boy as he came into our life as a gift. Tonya had been right. We were meant to adopt, and ready or not, we had two more sons coming.

The birth mother seemed relieved and resolved to take the next steps. She was healthy and far along with the other upcoming baby boy. We felt his presence as well and knew the two were meant to stay together and be with us. By the next day, the agency was working together with a district judge to get the paperwork put together and the due diligence and background checks done. The adoption proceedings were under way.

The legal details were handled quickly, and soon the day came for Zach to come home with us. The birth mother wanted to actually give Zach directly to us herself. We were happy to accommodate any wish she had to make the process easier for her. We had become aware of her deep love for her children. Her intention was not to "give them up" but to actually give them something better. This was the most selfless act I had ever seen anyone perform. It was not easy for her at all. We sat for nearly five hours as she mustered the courage to actually pass him to me. It was heart wrenching. I kept telling her we didn't have to go through with it all. We could simply all go home and forget it ever happened, but she insisted that it was for the best and was all meant to be. She said she knew the boys belonged with us. I knew the pain of losing a child. I also knew the agony of handing a child over to someone else. I had experienced that shortly after the accident in a profound dream about my son Griffin, who was killed. In my dream I actually stood in the presence of God and was granted the opportunity to "give" my son to Him so that I would not feel as if Griffin had been taken from me. The dream allowed me to exercise my will by saying good-bye to my son and turning him over to God. And while I was definitely not God, what we were experiencing with the young mother was no less poignant than my dream, and it was now playing out in reality.

Eventually, Zach fell asleep. While he was sleeping, his mother was able to kiss him on the face and hand him to me. I had a vivid flashback from my dream when I had handed my own son Griffin over to God. I felt such responsibility as I took my new son in my arms. I had been right there when the doctor delivered my other two boys, and this was no less sacred than when I took each of them into my arms for the first time. I felt the mother's pain in letting go and her trust and confidence in us becoming the parents to her child. It was overwhelming. Tears ran freely down all of our faces as the exchange was made. We committed to be in close contact with her until her unborn son came, and even beyond if she wished to.

The unconditional love we witnessed in her willingness to provide a better opportunity for her children above her own feelings was beyond words. Love at the deepest level. I had experienced that in the dream with my son Griffin, passing him over to what I knew was a greater good and higher cause. But my heart went out to this young mother having had not only the empathy of losing a child but also knowing what it felt like to give away a part of you that you love so deeply. I wept openly, holding Zach as she gathered her things and left the room to be alone and grieve.

chapter 15

Zach was now home. The love I felt for him was as strong as anything I had ever experienced with my own natural sons. My fears were soon alleviated as I realized that he was my boy. He had just come in a different way, but he was as much mine as my other sons.

There were still a lot of things to handle and adjustments to make. It was a huge adjustment for him and us. Spencer was key in grafting him in. They would play loud music and dance together, giggling and laughing until they were so exhausted they would just lie still on their backs, resting for a few min-

Shaving with Zach

utes before they started the whole ritual over again with a new song.

The birth mother remained local until the new baby was born. We began the process of selecting names for the unborn child. Tonya would research and write lists of names on sheets of paper in between caring for Spencer and Zach, which was a handful with the sudden presence of a toddler in the house. Everything had to be put away or upgraded for his safety: electrical plug guards, drawer stoppers, stairway gates, and on and on. Zach was into everything, and it was quite a leap into absolute free fall on Tonya's part. At least I had raised children before. She was a first timer and had jumped into the deep end without taking a deep breath.

The name that eventually stayed at the top of the list was Aiden. It was certainly my favorite. It is a Celtic name that means "little fire." It was perfect to me, not only because of the time I had spent in Scotland as a young man, but because I had a dream much like the dreams Tonya had been having during this crazy time of adoption and rebuilding a family.

In my dream I was in a wheat field, like the fields I grew up in. The sky was that violet color it becomes right at dusk, just before the sun falls behind the horizon. I stood quietly in the field, running my fingertips over the top of the soft, prickly beards of wheat. As I did so, I felt a hush come across the entire field and then saw two figures coming toward me, a woman and a child. As they came closer, I recognized the woman as Tamara, and the child as an older version of Griffin. He was now running and playing at the feet of his mother. He appeared to be about four years old, the age he would have been in this life had we not lost him in the auto accident. He hid shyly behind his mother as she came to a stop right in front of me. He clung to her white cotton skirt and peaked around her legs in a teasing manner. She smiled at me and said, "I wanted to show you something." She then reached around and gently pulled him in front of her. Cupping his face under his chin with her hands, he smiled a knowing smile at me. I knew it was Griffin, I felt his soul and our connection. He was beautiful.

As I looked at him deeply, feeling our spirits connect yet again, I actually saw the look of Zach in his eyes. His eyes were always that striking crystal blue, but it was only in this moment that I realized he and Zach had the same eyes, strong, beautiful blue eyes. I felt the connection I was developing with Zach. I knew, even though he was adopted, that he was much like me. I let all those feelings sink in, and as they did, another vision flashed before me in the dream. It was a quick little image, like a subliminal frame in a movie, but I saw it clearly. It was short but distinctive. I saw another little boy with radiant, almost orange, strawberry-blond hair. Although it was a quick glimpse, I knew this was the unborn child that was soon coming. I looked at Tamara, and she only smiled, acknowledging that I got the message.

As I awoke, I felt a deep love for Tonya and all she was doing and bringing into my life, even if it was frightening and on a fast track. I thought about what I had seen in the dream and the little boy with fire-colored hair. I knew his name would be Aiden, "little fire." It was perfect.

Several weeks after that dream the adoption agency called and explained that the delivery date was soon and that the birth mother had requested Tonya to be with her during the birth. Tonya was a little apprehensive, but I convinced her it would be a beautiful experience, so we agreed. A few days later the social worker from the adoption agency called us from her cell phone. They were en route to the hospital. Our birth mother was now in labor, and Aiden was on his way! At this point, our birth mother requested that I too join them in the birthing room. Now I understood Tonya's apprehension. I felt it was different since I was a man, but this time Tonya convinced me that we should both be there.

As the labor progressed, Tonya had joined the birth mother at her bedside and was holding her hand and feeding her ice chips. I, however, had found a seat at a comfortable distance away on the couch that was near the window of the birthing suite. As the labor became even more intense and progressive, the birth mother called for me to join them. I was confused and reluctant. She saw my hesitation and yelled in that guttural labor intense voice, "Are you the father of this child or not?"

"Yes, well no, but *yes*." I replied.

"Then get over here!" she said.

I joined her and Tonya as Aiden came into the world. It was amazing. In fact, the doctor actually put me in gloves at the request of both Tonya and the birth mother, and I got to catch Aiden, cut his umbilical cord, and be the first to hold him and welcome him into this world. I gave him his first little bath and then passed him on to his mothers. It was a beautiful experience. I had witnessed him coming into the world just like I had my natural sons. And though Griffin was gone, I felt him smiling on the situation from above, knowing Spencer would now have not only one but two brothers.

I walked for a while outside, breathing in the evening air. Life was moving so fast, but it felt like blessings were flowing my way. I had a grateful spirit as I looked at the stars. I was nervous and a bit overwhelmed, but grateful. I returned to get another look at Aiden. He was there in a blanket, dry from his bath and content. Sure enough, his hair had a definite orange tinge, and one look into his newborn eyes let me know he was the one I had seen in my dream. We brought him home. Tonya and I and our three boys set out to create a family.

chapter 16

*I*t was interesting for our three boys. They all had something in common. Each had a birth mother who was elsewhere. It was something that could later bond them, but I won't lie—it was mayhem. With one child you focus, with two you divide and conquer, with three, all hell breaks lose, and you simply hold on tight and try not to get bucked off.

With all the focus on marriage, family, and adoption, I had let things at the office slip. Our business was struggling. My personal savings had been gobbled up in the adoption fees. We were going through layoffs and intense pressures at work, which caused me financial concern. Tonya was frazzled at home juggling three kids that had all come at once. Between the stress at work, the sleep deprivation at home, and still actually working on my new marriage, I was barely holding it all together. I kept putting on a confident demeanor as if all was well, but it was a rugged adjustment. It had all happened so fast. It truly was like drinking from a fire hose.

Over the next few years everything was a blur. It was like a crazy dream with so many complicated parts and details that it simply became mush. I had received so many spiritual prompt-ings along the way and followed them. I expected things to fall into place when I did so, yet it all felt like such chaos. I was doing what I thought was right. Why wasn't it easy? Why wasn't life smoother? Why all the challenges and setbacks? Why wasn't it all working out the way I had envisioned it? I was falling into an abyss of self-doubt. My only answers were to work harder, pray harder, love more. I did all the things I thought would help, only to find I was still drowning in unmet expectations.

Tonya was not only dealing with the reality of jumping from single to married with three children in a whirlwind timeframe, but she was also shouldering the culture shock of moving into a tight-knit Mormon community. It was smothering her.

Our boys were all displaying issues as well. Spencer was becoming more and more introverted. Tonya was concerned enough to have him evaluated. I was in denial. I felt he was just depressed and working through all the adjustments in his life, but Tonya knew there was more to it. She wanted to have him tested to make sure he was all right. When we took him to a specialist, we learned what I had viewed as an interesting personality was actually diagnosed as Asperger's syndrome, a high-functioning form of autism. Zach was suffering from attachment disorder and was displaying such horrible temper tantrums and fits that we sought assistance from the Children's Center at the university, a special every day program for preschoolers with behavior issues. The level of his emotional and even physical distress was consistently so intense that we were concerned for his well-being. Aiden was a demanding baby and displayed signs of what was eventually diagnosed as severe ADHD. It wasn't just raising three boys, but taking on special children, each of which had unique characteristics to be dealt with. The dynamic of all three together compounded our stress and caused much worry and restlessness. The demands at work continued to be stressful as well—managing demanding clients and deadlines and working to maintain the financial obligations of a small company during a severe economic downturn were all eating away at my contentment.

I found myself sometimes asking the "why" questions again. Why this? Why now? I had been through so much and had gained a great deal of spiritual insights, but I was obviously still learning. Returning home on a regular basis after horrific days at work to find Tonya broken down, crying in bed, and the boys creating an emotional three-ring circus was depressing. I wondered what was happening. I felt guilty, as if I had somehow talked Tonya into marrying me and made her miserable. I felt bad that she had taken on so much. Granted, it was all her choice, but I felt responsible for her happiness, and she didn't seem happy. I would imagine that perhaps I should have stayed single and just raised Spencer on my own. Then the guilt of the car crash would return, and I would feel as if I had ruined his life in some way as well. I would look at my two adopted little boys and feel there must be thousands of better fathers out there for them than me.

Even as a man I struggled. My physical pain was constant, and though I worked through it day after day to provide a living, I felt as if Tonya deserved a whole man, not a crippled one. A man with two legs and not all the injuries and pain I dealt with. And what of my heart? It was still broken too. I knew deep down I was still grieving in many ways, but I didn't dare talk about it with anyone. I was afraid to share my grief, struggles, or feelings. I had moved on, right? I had remarried and adopted two beautiful babies. What was there to grieve? Why could I not just be grateful? But the emotional pain hadn't gone away. I even felt guilty about that. Why couldn't I quit hurting inside and just let it go? But I kept it in and hid my pain from everyone. I wasn't comfortable talking about it, and I carried false expectations about how to find its remedy. I expected Tonya to fix it. I expected the boys to fix it. I expected my career to fix it. I was looking for anyone to simply validate me and make me feel better about myself. I was trying so hard to make everything work, yet my children were having issues, Tonya was struggling with her new life, and I—I was grasping for what I knew was true, what I knew I had experienced spiritually, but it hadn't manifested itself it the way I thought it would.

We decide to sell the house and make a fresh start. We wanted to reset everything somewhere as simply "the Olsens," not the widower and his son, the new bride, and two adopted kids. Our family deserved unity but didn't have it. It was also tough to create unity with so many onlookers waiting and wondering what would become of the puzzle pieces.

The house sold relatively quickly, but we priced it to sell in a buyer's market, which didn't vastly improve our finances. We found a "fixer-upper" rambler across the street from the junior high school Spencer would soon be attending. We poured all our energy into the little house and made a beautiful home out of it. It was good to start fresh in a new neighborhood with unfamiliar surroundings and new people to meet.

Over time, things at work began to improve. The boys were all doing better as well. Spencer mainstreamed into seventh grade, Zach transitioned out of the Children's Center, and under the direction of physicians, we were managing Aiden's ADHD relatively well.

Tonya and I still had work to do, however. Somewhere in the middle of bawling kids, messy diapers, and the constant stress, I had lost her. I had lost myself. I had lost the magic of our relationship and how we came together. I was still looking for external validation from the outside in, instead of from the inside out. I felt disjointed in many ways. I still had so many pieces to put back together within myself. I was constantly, secretly searching for comfort and validation. I wanted wholeness. I wanted light. I wanted to feel that I was okay, that we were okay, and that I had made all the right decisions. There was a massive hollow in my heart that could not be filled. Not by anyone.

Although I was rebuilding a family, I had not rebuilt myself. I was only finding ways to dress the wound and would have to go much deeper to ever find true healing.

chapter 17

I *knew the best way to get over feeling sorry for* myself was to serve others. At the time of the accident, when I was so severely injured tht my spirit actually left my body briefly, I experienced something profound. When out of the body, a veil was lifted. I saw people differently. I saw them with no judgment, only unconditional love. I knew them at such a deep level and experienced the oneness and connection we all share. I wanted to feel that way again. I wanted to see others as God saw them. I wanted to see myself as God saw me. I decided to re-create in some way my experience, if I could, and the cherry tree in the backyard of our rambler house was the perfect opportunity.

Spencer and I went out and picked several five-gallon buckets of fresh cherries from the large tree in our backyard. We washed them and bagged them into quart-sized ziplock bags. I knew even if we froze most of them that we would never be able to eat them all ourselves, so we created a game of the situation. We decided to sit down and listen to our hearts so we'd be guided as to who might be most deserving of the fresh cherries. As I sat quietly a simple verse came into my heart: "I was a stranger and ye took me in." Then the prompting hit me. What if we actually took the cherries to strangers instead of friends and neighbors? We'd close our eyes and just practice feeling inspiration as to where to go with the cherries, and then who to give them to. We drove around giving the cherries to random folks all along the way. They laughed and were grateful. Some were a bit apprehensive, but most were taken aback and warmed by the randomness and the kindness. We eventually ended up near my office in downtown Salt Lake City, still armed with several bags of cherries.

At one point, we were driving along the west side of Pioneer Park when Spencer asked me to stop. I pulled the truck off to the side of the road. He closed his eyes for a while, and then he opened them and told me he got the message. He got out of the truck and headed toward a rough-looking homeless man sitting in the park. Needless to say, I was apprehensive as a father, but I just kept a close eye on him as he approached the man and held out the cherries. I watched them exchange in a brief conversation. The man took the cherries and held the ziplock bag as if it were sacred as they talked some more. The man eventually buried his head in his hands and started quivering with sobbing gestures as Spencer ran back toward the truck.

I asked him what had happened. He told me the man reminisced about his home and his mother. The man told him they had a big cherry tree in their yard when he was a little boy and that the cherries reminded him of his mom. This was a big lesson for both of us and something I really needed. I wanted to give myself a break from the day to day and get back in touch with spiritual things, remembering my connection to divine things and that by putting all judgments aside and simply following our hearts, we created miracles.

Something as simple as a ziplock bag of cherries became a cherished gift and memory, a link from a broken life to a loving past. It was also a vivid reminder that we are all connected. By simply opening up my heart and operating from pure love,

Spencer and I had created little miracles all around us. I also knew I had all my own answers within myself if I chose to seek them. By simply being still and listening to that little voice that speaks to the heart, and then trusting it, we had known exactly where to be, what to say, and whom to speak to in every moment.

I wanted every day to be like that. I wanted to do that in my home life too. It was one thing to go out and engage with strangers for an afternoon, but what about those times at home when it was difficult and challenges came up? Would I implement my heart then and know what to say and how to handle every situation? I was still struggling greatly with my own inner wounds. Spreading healing to others was good, and watching Spencer enjoy the bliss of doing that was good too, but I still wasn't connecting the experience to my own painful past and personal healing. I wanted someone to bring me the fresh cherries, the fruit that would give me a brighter outlook on life and true inner healing.

My mistake was expecting someone else to deliver the fruit to me. My pain was in counting on others to fill my inner void. I wanted to feel that same love we were creating that afternoon, but I was forgetting the only one who could create it for me was me. I was so busy battling to put all of my personal puzzle pieces back together that I was missing the big picture of what I was really trying to create. If I wanted to experience this same love, peace, and joy, then I had to embrace it from within myself. How could I expect to give what I did not have, and how was I to find it with the huge hole still in my heart?

I worried about my boys. Would I ever be the father they deserved? I worried about Tonya. Would I ever be the husband she dreamed of? Although I created brief moments of light through community service, connecting with my sons, and spending quiet time alone, I felt I was slipping into darkness. Nothing I did on the outside would bring enough light to heal me from the inside. I was drowning in self-loathing and insecurities about everything— about me being enough for Tonya and the boys, my ability to provide for them, my capacity to juggle work and civil activities that seemed to be multiplying daily. I even began to doubt my connection to God and to my angels. I was going through the motions, sleepwalking, but forgetting who I really was and my connection to light.

chapter 18

The months and years rolled on, and our boys each grew in personality and did so with joy, but each had

Spencer

their major challenges. Spencer became very interested in music. He was playing in several bands and was becoming a talented musician. It was a wonderful way for him to express himself nonverbally, since verbal communication was sometimes difficult for him. As adolescence came, the sweet, shy supportive child had become an angry young man. Spencer struggled at times in his relationship with Tonya. He struggled to fit in socially as well. At least music provided him with a like-minded peer group through high school, but I wondered about the influences he was attracting to himself. He was into pretty heavy, dark music and had become more and more reclusive.

Zach became our athletic child, excelling in sports but struggling to find his place. He didn't enjoy sports and felt I was forcing him to participate in them. I wasn't. I enjoyed watching and coaching him, but he only felt it as pressure from me to excel. I feared he only saw my enthusiasm as an unreachable expectation of some kind. He was resentful and tried to distance himself from me. He later found his true passion in musical theater, dance, and drama. I was enthusiastic and supportive of that as well but knew too little about it to connect with him beyond watching.

Aiden was the family comedian. His sense of humor and wit were beyond his years, but they were often inappropriate. Humor was his coping mechanism to fit in. He was closely connected with Spencer but was growing up way too fast, trying to fit in with him and his high school friends. He was funny, and kept us all laughing with his silly impressions and antics. I suppose laughter was good between the tears.

With our boys' difficulties came my own. Tonya and I had become disconnected. We had given everything to our children, to maintaining the house and to my career, and yet so little to each other. We didn't talk, touch, or really connect to each other at all. We had lost our intimacy, not just physically, but emotionally as well. That candle we left burning on that little table on my country bridge years ago was barely flickering. The constant storm had diminished it to only a flicker.

As Spencer graduated and left for college, a piece of me left with him. I realized that so much of my energy had been wrapped up in him, making up for the guilt I felt over the crash. The hole in my heart seemed to expand even larger when he moved out. The emptiness he had been filling was void too. Reality hit me right in the face. Had I done enough to raise him strong? Was he aware enough to be a man and make good decisions? Had my secret self-doubt and insecurities translated to him vicariously in any way? Had I been a good enough father and taught him well? It was too late to correct any of that now. He was leaving and might never live under our roof again. The bleakness was that I was now out of time and all I could do had already been done, yet it had blown by in a blur.

As Spencer left, I thought about my own life and when I left for college. I thought about what drove me during those volatile years when I was not even a man but thought I knew about life. And yet what life had taught me was that things didn't always work out. People were hard to trust. I could only count on myself, yet deep down, I felt I didn't measure up. In truth it was only my insecurities that had driven me. The feeling that I was not good enough, and a desire to prove to everyone somehow that I was, had been my biggest motivator. It seemed like a sickness as I looked back on it, yet here I was still living that way: feeling so small, striving for all kinds of accolades and recognition, not only at work but also from Tonya and anyone else who would throw them my way. It was all a bandage to my own feelings of inadequacy. And no one knew—no one but me. It was my big secret. Even after all I had experienced, I still needed others to tell me I was okay.

I wondered where all those insecurities came from. Where did this all start? Why did I have such an inferiority complex? I actually broke down at the office after working late one night after everyone had gone. I cried out to God, and for the first time in many years it was sincere. "Why God?" I cried aloud. "What's wrong with me? Why do I feel this way? Why is there never enough? Why can nothing fill my emptiness and need?"

There was silence. I heard and felt nothing, which left me empty and searching. I wondered if I would have to simply draw from my earlier answers and the spiritual things I had experienced at the time of the accident. It seemed so long ago. So far away, yet I could not deny what I had felt, seen, and experienced, but why not now? I felt so alone. Why had God forgotten me now? Had I messed up my life beyond his reach? In my quest to truly become nonjudgmental, had I lost all good judgment? There had been so many choices that didn't work. So much heartache and let downs. And I had let so many down in so many ways, mostly my family, and myself. Letting myself down was the most painful.

In the spring of that year I finally came to Tonya in a broken heap and poured out all my shame and pain. Confessing my deepest regrets, I shared with her how I felt, my sorrow, my grief, my feelings of insecurity, my anger, and my misery—all the parts of my life that didn't work.

I expected her to turn me away and realize that I was different than the strong mask I had always put on. However, through it all, she simply showed me love. She accepted me in spite of it all. Everything I had hid from her in fear of her seeing me as bad, weak, small, or inadequate. She forgave all of it. She freely forgave everything that for so long I had been holding against myself. It was a miracle.

My mind rushed back in time to when I first met her and how I fell in love with her. The promptings I was given right from the beginning of our relationship, including the experience I had at Tamara's grave. When I felt her so near and was told that Tonya would teach me to love unconditionally. All these years through the struggles I thought I was learning to love her unconditionally, when in reality I was actually being taught by her unconditional love for me. She had always loved me. It was I who didn't love myself. Tamara had been right on. Tonya would teach me unconditional love, by putting me in situations where I would finally learn to fully love myself.

It was such a powerful and profound experience. That little candle we had started burning on that stormy night of our engagement so long ago was now burning brightly again. The wind and rain only made it stronger and more determined to radiate light into our darkness, and that light changed everything, yet the only thing that had changed was me. The situations were all the same. The boys and their challenges, my work and its demands, our relationship and the intricacies of piecing a family back together, it was all still there. My perspective, however, had changed, and that was the miracle.

Peace had come, finally. All these years I had beat myself up over so many things. I had doubted my choices and blamed myself when things didn't go splendidly. I had spent so many sleepless nights lying awake, wondering and listening to the voices in my head. I spent so many hours at work avoiding what was happening at home. But now, peace was here, light was here. I finally rested in a way that I hadn't in so long. I did often wish I could go back and start all over again. I wanted to reverse time and do things differently with what I knew now. Tonya deserved this newer, whole me from the beginning of our relationship.

I drifted into sleep one night not long after all this with the notion that I really wanted a complete fresh start with Tonya without all we had been through. As I slept, Tamara actually came to me in another dream. She ran up and put her arms around my neck. She swung around me, dancing joyfully, and kissed me on my face. Then she stopped twirling and looked me right in the eyes. She spoke but only said this simple phrase, "All that exists here is wisdom." That's all she said. But then she continued to look at me and communicate without words. A flood of knowledge flowed between us. She communicated that it didn't matter what I had done or what I didn't do. All that mattered was what I had learned from it. All that existed in the heavenly realms was wisdom. My burdens could be made light, not as in less heavy, but actually by being illuminated into *light*. My choices, and the results of those choices, were only there for me to learn from, and those lessons simply brought about wisdom. It had all been a blessing. There was no reason to go back. No reason for deep regret for things I could not now change. We had created the experience together and now stood on higher ground. We could start fresh from right there and move forward without having to erase what in reality had brought us wisdom. We could honor the lesson without judging the process that provided it.

I awoke with a fresh, new heart. The hole in me seemed much smaller now. Tonya hadn't filled it. Even Tamara and the dream had not filled it, but *I* was finally filling it. I was finally validating myself. The light was within me, and always had been. I had just turned it off and forgotten.

chapter 19

After my dream, I once again found myself asking God where all the insecurities had come from, except in a much different spirit this time. I wasn't angrily demanding answers, but trusting in God and knowing He was there for me.

"Why God? When did this all start?" I asked. "Why have I lived a life of feeling so inadequate, even though I am enough? Where did all the insecurities come from?"

As smoothly as I asked, the answers flowed into my understanding. I actually saw myself vividly in my mind's eye. I was four years old behind the coach in my childhood home. My mom and dad were splitting up, and I didn't know why. Divorce wasn't something I could comprehend. I only knew that what I had trusted to be true and forever wasn't. I watched as the little boy's heart broke. I saw him, me, heaving with sobs and emotions, this perfect little boy, innocent, breaking as his world crumbled before him.

I looked at my four-year-old self. I recognized those little boy hands, those hand-me-down jeans, and that hair, how Mom had trimmed it over the ears and across the forehead with her sewing scissors on the back porch of the house. I looked on as he sobbed, knowing it was me, and feeling his pain but from my current adult perspective. I was compelled to go to him, so I did. It was as real and vivid as if I were really doing it. I bent down by that smaller, earlier version of myself, and I picked him up and held him. I comforted that child. I felt his little hands on my own neck as I wiped his tears and we made eye contact. I assured him that he was okay, that everything would turn out all right. He smiled, and I remembered that crooked little-boy smile. I was hugging me!

"It all turns out, you know. We are only here to learn. All that exists is wisdom." I said to my little self.

And love, I thought as the much younger, much smaller me leaned into my chest and stopped crying.

All these years I had carried all that pain and insecurity. But now it was gone. The key was that the healing had always been up to me. I had had the answers all along.

As quickly as life had seemed to spiral out of control, it was now ascending into something so new. It felt so different to be with Tonya now. We fell in love all over again. It didn't take big things. We now simply made time for each other. We really looked at each other. We connected. We listened. We touched. We even played Yahtzee from time to time. I was healing from within. I was offering her a whole man, no matter what body parts were missing. All these years I had expected her to meet me in the middle. I had thought that if I gave fifty percent she would give fifty, and we would somehow create a whole. But now I was whole on my own. I no longer needed her validation, nor anyone else's. I had my own power, my own light. I was bringing one hundred percent to the table. I needed no one. Now, I simply chose her. There was no need or expectations. Only love, which I could give freely because I was finally beginning to love myself.

My focus returned to my own boys and how I could show up for them in more powerful ways. Spencer had been struggling at school to find his faith and answers. His grades were high but his emotions low, and he was wading through his own darkness in many ways. Zach was experiencing sadness over being adopted and had been searching for his own identity in many ways. Aiden was having a difficult time focusing enough in school to learn what was expected and was falling behind.

I was looking forward to the summer months and taking a break from all of it just to reconnect with Tonya and the boys. We planned a weekend trip to the family cabin for fishing on the lake, hiking in the hills, and basically checking out and unplugging from the world for a while.

The weather was beautiful, and we enjoyed being with

Fishing with Aiden

family and in nature. Tonya relaxed in the sun by the lake with her sisters-in-law while I fished with Aiden. Zach and his cousins all went swimming and playing in the shallow end of the water. Spencer took a four-wheeler on one of the small mountain trails to explore and clear his head.

Everyone was doing what he or she loved while resting and interacting with extended family. It felt like heaven was right here on earth—the smell of fresh trees and the lake in the air sprinkled by the laughter of dear ones, the random hawk in flight or elk wandering into the meadow. For the first time in a long time I felt peace. My heart was finally right, and that rippled out into everything around me.

chapter 20

On the evening of our second day we gathered in the cabin around a roaring fire for dinner. My younger brother, Justin, was grilling the catch of the day out on the deck while the rest of us set the table and debated which card games to play after dinner. The only one missing was Spencer.

As it became darker I began to worry a bit about where he might be. He had been out on the four-wheeler all day. I was sure he knew his way back but wondered, as it got dark, why he hadn't returned. I was concerned if something had happened or if he had run out of gas or something. The cell service was poor in the mountains, and he would have no way of reaching us if something had gone wrong.

We were just about to go out looking for him when he pulled up. He was quiet and looked concerned.

"I want to talk to you, Dad," he said sternly as he parked the four-wheeler and entered the cabin.

"Come in, son. Sit down," I replied.

"No, Dad, I want to talk to you in private."

I walked out onto the porch and asked what was going on.

"Can we go for a ride or something away from everyone?" He answered.

It was already dark and getting cold, so I grabbed the truck keys and beckoned him to climb in. We drove down the trail and onto the main road in silence.

"What's up, son?" I asked

"I don't know. I just need to talk."

"What's on your mind?"

Spencer sat silently looking out the window into the darkness. My heartbeat quickened as I wondered what he might say. He was hard to read. At least he was willing to talk to me, if he would.

He sat still, just gazing out the window. I pulled the truck off the dirt lane and sat, waiting for him to speak.

"I don't know what to think, Dad," he started in soft, unsure tones. "I don't know if I believe you."

I swallowed hard.

"How so, son? I've never lied to you."

"You speak of a God who loves us. You speak of these profound experiences and dreams you have. You talk about healing and answers. I don't get any of that!"

I sat silently not knowing what to say and watched as he became more emotional.

"You speak of having peeked into heaven, of leaving your body after the crash. You speak of saying good-bye to Mom and Griffin. You speak of how they come to you in dreams and visions. I've never had any of that. In fact, that's where I was today. I went out on the four-wheeler to find a secluded place. I knew that here, in this peaceful place, I could get an answer. I poured my heart out all day. I begged God for a feeling or anything, but nothing came. I wanted proof or some kind of sign."

As I listened, I felt my own eyes moisten as tears began to roll down his cheeks.

"There was nothing, Dad. Nothing! For twelve years I have begged God to just let me see Mom, even once. For twelve years

I begged God to allow me to feel something. Anything! But there has been nothing. And today again, I went in full faith. I knew if God were there, he would give me an answer. I poured my whole soul out for hours today into the evening, but nothing came. Nothing. Just emptiness. So either you're deceived in some way, or if God is there, he certainly doesn't care about me!"

He fell over against the window and started to cry, my six-foot-two young man breaking down and becoming emotional.

I sat watching. All I could do was put my hand on his shoulder. He sat up and wiped his eyes and nose with his hand. He looked right at me.

"I'm done with it, Dad. I'm done with believing. I've lost my faith. I want nothing to do with religion or any of it. I've begged almost every day for years and never have I experienced anything. You've had all these beautiful experiences. You've seen all these things, but for me, it's been nothing like that."

His face fell back into his hands. My tears now flowed too as I felt the intensity of his pain. I didn't know what to say.

He leaned back against the window again, and I put my hand back on his shoulder.

I knew he wasn't mad at me; he was mad at God and was telling me about it openly and honestly. I wasn't mad at him either. This was the little boy who had been so supportive. He had loved me so much. When I came home so broken physically and spiritually after nearly five months in the hospital, he told me he would love me "even if I was nothing but a puddle of blood." Now he was questioning me and doubting my experiences. At least he was talking to me. I still didn't know what to say. I had experienced the things I had shared with him, but knowing he had petitioned for so long, for anything, with no answer, hurt me almost as deeply as it did him.

He gained his composure and we sat there in the darkness. There was nothing to say. I wondered why I had received the experiences I had. I'd give them all away for him to have some kind of "knowing" of his own. I wondered why some people have spiritual things happen and others don't. It obviously has nothing to do with our willingness or being deserving. Why me and not my innocent child? I thought of all those nights when Spencer as a little boy went to his room, and unbeknownst to me, begged God to send him any kind of comfort. I thought of those dark nights in his adolescence when he was so open but the door to heaven remained shut. I wondered about nights like this in his early adult life when even in his faith and willingness, nothing came in spite of his cries. Why did God provide experiences for some and not for others?

I had no answer for him. Even as his mortal father, I had no comfort to give beyond just sitting there hurting with him. It wasn't fair. What about life ever is? I blessed him in the only way I knew how to as a father. We sat for a while, and when we had both gained our composure, I mustered up the only words that could come to mind.

"Sometimes when we seek signs, the signs never come. And there never may be a burning bush or thunder and lightning from the sky, but I know what I experienced was real. And I also know your answers will come to you at some point. It will be in a special way and at a special time, and probably when you least expect it, but it will be just for you. It may be a simple hushed whisper in your heart or a gentle subtle feeling in the air, but I know Mom and Griff will let you know they're there. And in knowing they're there, you'll know God is there too, and that He loves you."

He looked at me uncertainly.

"Okay, I'll make you a deal," I said. "If and when I die, I will come to you. I will come to you in some way that you will know it's me and it will be undeniable. Okay?"

That's all I could say. There was nothing to prove or convince him of. There would never be any proof anyway, but I wanted him to find his own light. I didn't want him living on my faith

Spencer

and my experiences. I wanted him to find his own answers, even if they weren't mine. It went far beyond him finding religion. I wanted him to find peace. I simply wanted him to be happy.

chapter 21

On Sunday afternoon we all went our separate ways. Spencer headed north to Logan, and Tonya and I went home with the younger boys.

I did a lot of soul searching about our conversation. The soul searching took me on quite a journey, everything from studying spiritual modalities like Reiki and spending time with Native American shamans to doing intense experiential trainings. I delved much deeper into my own faith and embraced its symbols on a much higher level. I really began praying again, trusting and listening. I read and reread a lot of good books—all of which served me well. I asked God to touch Spencer in some way that he could comprehend. I called upon our deceased loves ones to come to him. I now begged for my son to receive assistance from heaven in some kind of meaningful way, like I had. And if Spencer didn't want religion, perhaps he could obtain spirituality and direction in his own quiet way, which felt even more important to me than anything else.

After our trip, I began to have more vivid dreams, and more often. One night before bed, I was contemplating Spencer's path and found that I was actually on a renewed path of my own. I began pondering on the notion of religion versus spirituality and how it all fit. I was beginning to see a strong thread of truth that ran throughout so many aspects of my own life and came from so many diverse sources. My last conscious thought as I drifted off to sleep was that the role of any religion was to assist one in reaching personal spirituality. However, no matter the religion, powerful personal spirituality was the desired end goal. I faded off into a deep sleep.

As I slept I had a vivid dream. In this dream I was shown three people. I was first shown Gandhi, whom I knew little about except for the few things I had learned in history classes. I was shown his life: how he lived, what he did, and how he loved. I was shown his religion, Hinduism, and what it meant to him and how he embraced the traditions and symbols of his personal culture and beliefs. It was inspiring. He was wonderful.

I was then shown a woman. Mother Teresa of Calcutta, a Christian, a Catholic nun. I was shown her life. How she lived. How she loved. I was shown her religion and what it meant to her—her traditions and symbols and the beauty she found within them.

I was then shown Jesus, a Jewish man practicing his Jewish ceremonies and symbols throughout his life, right up until the end. I was shown how he lived: what he did, how he loved, and what he stood for. I was shown his religion and what it meant to him. The power he found in the traditions and symbols of his culture. It was beautiful.

As the vision of these three astounding individuals came to an end, a voice in the dream said this to me: "It was not their religion that gave them power. Their power came in knowing who they were and in their connection to the Creator." I realized that in knowing that, they lived and loved in divine ways, and so could I.

These three distinctive people from three diverse cultures and theologies were unified in the way they loved and their knowledge of their divine connection to our divine source.

After that, I embraced my own religion in much more meaningful ways. I began to see the deeper beauty in my own symbols and ceremonies. I saw profound, symbolic meaning in my own religious ordinances that I hadn't before. And in the same breath, truth became far more important to me than religion. I knew I could fully embrace my culture, my traditions, and my faith, but my power was truly found in a personal connection and direct communication with my Divine Creator.

I wanted Spencer, and our entire family, to find that same truth. My experiences over the years had transformed my hope and faith into absolute trust. I knew that whatever my circumstances, those circumstances were perfect for my soul's progression. I let go of my expectations of what things were supposed to look like and trusted God. I trusted the process, which I knew was customized and designed perfectly for me individually. And if my experience here was in such good hands, then I knew all those around me were in those same good hands. Even Spencer. Especially Spencer.

For so long I had hovered over him as a father. Protecting him, making his decisions, seeing that he did what I thought he was supposed to do. My motivation was love, and I simply wanted him to be happy and succeed, but that was quickly shifting. I was now able to respect and honor him as a man, a man that could make his own decisions and then learn from the consequences of his choices. After all, isn't that what God does with all of us? Grants us free will and choice and then lovingly allows us to learn and grow from the experience of our choices? We thereby are accountable in the end for what we created and how we grow from it. There is no finger pointing, blame, or judgment.

It is a beautiful process. For so long I had adopted the constrictive philosophy that making him obey me so he wouldn't experience pain or get lost was the way to go. But that didn't serve either of us. Our spirits are free and only grow when we are given the wings to fly and learn from our own experiences.

By letting go of my judgment I could actually see him now in his magnificence as a young man while no longer holding him in smallness as a helpless child. He was not helpless, nor had he ever been. He was a strong and noble soul simply going through the process of defining who he was.

I also knew that experience is the only true teacher. I thought of my own adolescence and early adulthood. I recalled all those long chalkboard talks in the high school and college football locker rooms. In theory, every play was a touchdown or stopped at the line of scrimmage depending on your perspective of offense or defense. I remembered watching all those game films and theorizing about how it was done and what would work. But I had no idea how fast a four-point-four-second forty was until I was actually on the field, doing it, experiencing it. That was the only way to really grow. I got knocked around a lot and missed some tackles, but boy did I learn from it. In the meantime I made a few plays as well, and that felt good, but the more intense learning often came from really messing up. Life is like that. It's our greatest teacher. The things we experience here and the truths we take to heart from those experiences are all that really matters. They are the wisdom we get to keep.

I began to trust that Spencer would find his way, as would all of us, but it would be in his way and might look completely different than my way, or Tonya's, his brothers', or anyone else's in this world for that matter. And that was okay. In fact, it finally all made perfect sense.

chapter 22

I *knew Spencer was on his perfect path, but I* still wondered why some people have spiritual experiences and others don't. I experienced so many dreams, visions, and insights and had so many angels assisting me along the way. There seemed to be no rhyme or reason to it at all. There was no qualifier, no consistency in circumstances—only the simple fact that some people, for no apparent reason, have profound spiritual encounters, and others, for no apparent reason, do not. Why had I been granted the things I experienced without even asking and Spencer had experienced nothing after begging for years?

The answer remained the same. It was all part of the perfect experience for our individual growth and development. If someone were to have spiritual experiences, it would be because that is exactly what is best for that person to grow, and if others do not, then that is perfect for their path and spiritual growth, neither one being the right or wrong way to experience this life. Extraordinary things may or may not happen, but putting expectations on the outcome of another's spiritual path is only placing judgment on each individual's experience. Every soul's experience is customized. And if customized specifically for them, what right do I have to judge it? Judgment and comparison only brought me pain.

As I pondered these profound truths, my mind wandered back to Spencer, his faith and individuality. He was diving into a process of literally manifesting who and what he chose to be. He too was soul searching, reading a lot, pondering, doing intense trainings, and was being very open to whatever he might learn. He was looking into diverse ideas and then feeling what was true for him. He was simply walking his path. So I decided to walk with him, from a distance, without hovering, judging, or feeling like I had to save him. I was simply loving and honoring who and what he chose to be, supporting the concept of individual free will and choice.

Eventually everything shifted in a dramatic fashion. It was not without hard work, but Spencer did find his own powerful answers. By the end of that summer, he came to me again, this time not in private. Tonya was with me. He was every bit as sober as the first time and with even more tears, but now he came with tears of joy. He gave me a big bear hug and just held on. While still embracing me, he said, "I love you Dad and I believe you. It's all

Tonya, Spencer, and Jeff

real. Mom's there, and it's all okay. I know what I know now, and nobody can ever take that away."

I pulled back to look at him. All I saw was pure joy. I saw that happy little boy who Spencer had been before the crash, but now in a young man's body. His eyes were filled with light, and his smile was illuminated. I didn't have to ask what had happened. Somehow I already knew. He then turned to Tonya and actually cupped her face in his hands. He looked her right in the eye, which he hadn't done for so long. "I love you," he said. "Thank you for everything you have done for me. For coming to us and being my mom."

That uncorked my emotions, and my own tears flowed freely. We all stood there, clinging to each other, and wept for joy. The most beautiful part is it had nothing to do with me. My son had experienced his own miracle, and he created it for himself. It was the most satisfying thing as a father to know that he didn't need me. He had become a man with all his own answers.

It's the wish of every father that his children grow up better than he is, that they stand on their own two feet and be independently strong. I didn't realize until that moment that I was inadvertently raising my sons to never need me again. But that was the end goal. And that's exactly what I was witnessing in this sacred moment.

Making staffs with Spencer

I watched him continue to mature during the next year. We grew together. We spent time together, studied together, trained together, and talked a lot. On one occasion, one of Spencer's friends had gone to jail on drug charges. He was having a court hearing of some kind. Spencer announced to me that he would be attending the hearing in support of his friend. In my judgment I said, "You will not! You're not going to be associated with known drug dealers." He looked at me in surprise.

"Is that how it is, Dad? Is that how it's going to be? When somebody messes up, we turn our backs on them, ignore them? I'm going to go and stand with my friend. I may be the only one there to say, 'It's okay, I'm here for you and we'll get through this.'"

I knew he was right. I was actually proud of him for standing up to me. I realized then that he had always been a teacher to me. From the time he was born until now he had come as a mentor, a leader, and a light to my own path. Even when I felt he was lost and going through darkness, it had actually served as a backward way of showing me the light. I wondered if his spirit was wiser and older than mine and I was just catching up. There seemed to be such cosmic order to all that was happening and had happened.

My heart expanded to my other sons. I looked forward to what they would create of their lives. My thoughts turned to my little late son, Griffin. I wondered what part he must be playing in all of this. I longed for him. Each time my thoughts turned to him, I wondered what might have been—and what perhaps, in reality, was—based on knowing he was there somehow, looking down on it all.

I dreamt of Griffin that night as I slept. It was one of those strange lucid dreams where I can't truthfully say whether I was asleep or awake. It was the strangest dream. I sat there on the front seat of my dad's old white pickup truck. I remembered the truck in every detail. As I looked down, I realized I was wearing a toddler's jumpsuit, the kind that has the snaps all along the inner legs for easy diaper access. It was red corduroy. I followed the corduroy down my legs to see that I was wearing little white toddler lace-up shoes. I remembered this! *I was a baby*, I thought, as I took in all the details. *I remember being here, being small and wearing this.* I looked out the window and noticed I was in the pasture at our Wallsburg ranch. The Black Angus beef cattle were all crowding against the truck to get at the feed in the truck bed. I remembered this. I sat, becoming frightened because in my toddler mind I thought the cattle might tip the truck over or get inside somehow. I began to feel uneasy when suddenly the cattle scattered and my dad jumped into the cab of the truck with me. He comforted me. It was like I was there experiencing it all over again. I couldn't have been more than fourteen months old. Then it hit me: fourteen months old. That's the age Griffin was when I lost him in the crash. That's the age he was when he passed away, and here I was experiencing a moment from my life when I was that age. *Griffin*, I thought, and I looked out the truck window in my dream. As I did so, the truck, the cattle, and my dad all vanished, and I was suddenly my current age. Standing in front of me was my son Griffin, except he was not a fourteen-month-old at all. He stood before me as a full-grown twenty-something-year-old man. I recognized him immediately as my son. It was like looking in the mirror. He was so like me in features and build but taller and more muscular. He was magnificent. My son. Griffin. I wanted to rush to him, but his gaze stopped me. He looked directly in my eyes, and the nonverbal communication that so often takes place in my dreams began. Without using words he communicated to me, "I wanted you to remember this so that you would know that I will always remember being your son. I will always remember having you as my dad."

His gaze softened, and I was then able to rush to him. I threw my arms around him and leaned my head into his strong jaw. He embraced me back and we hugged tightly, heart to heart, for what felt like a few minutes. Then he did speak, right into my ear. "I have a message for you," he said. My spirit leaped with joy, a message from heaven from my son. I expected something profound and prophetic as I leaned into him to get the message.

"I love you, Dad. And I'm proud of you."

That was a far simpler and far more powerful message than anything to me. Here I had struggled, loved, worked with, ached over, and had so much joy in my living sons, but I was now communing with the son I lost, he now being a grown, powerful, magnificent man. What a perfect gift.

I awoke from the dream with my eyes still wet. Was it real or just a dream? It didn't matter. It was real to me, and that was all that mattered. To me, the dream showed that we are always connected, no matter what side of the veil we may be on. I learned that even the little things we do as parents matter. That the moments we create are eternal. I learned that memories are sacred and important. I learned that no matter what my shortcomings as a father might be, my love will always come through. I didn't need to be super dad to make a difference. I simply got to love my children. Loving them may be no grander than simply showing up and being there when they wanted a dad. It wasn't about being their friend, but about being their father.

The Olsen boys

It was about trust, not just them trusting me but me trusting them to grow, make choices, and learn. My job was to love them and let them know they were safe to live their lives and be magnificent in wisdom, which would come from experiencing many things. So I honored their experiences in perfect unconditional love, just as I knew my own had been honored.

chapter 23

My dreams have continued, vivid and poignant and always with a connection and a message. Some say it's a gift I brought back with me from my near-death experience in the car crash many years ago. Others say that having crossed over once before opens channels for me to receive such things easier. It doesn't matter to me the cause or the reason. I am simply grateful to have the insights.

I sometimes hesitate to share them so openly. I fully realize that many lose loved ones and never experience dreams or spiritual comfort at all. I know others have immense challenges in life without the support of family, friends, or glimpses from the other side. I also realize that I have been lucky. I don't share these things to make myself special in any way. None of us is special, yet we all are. I simply share them to assist others to heal. To comfort them in some way with the answers I've received, that they might find their own answers, in their own way.

I've come a long way since mile marker 80. What began there is still unfolding in my life in magnificent ways. I've learned so much. I've learned that there is always a choice, in everything. I've learned that I am completely accountable for my experience here. The universe does nothing to me. It lovingly supports me, without judgment, as I make my choices and grow.

I've learned that the masters of living connected to the Creator (Jesus, Gandhi, Mother Teresa, and so on) have only one message for us, that we are loved beyond measure. Jesus didn't come to show us how wonderful he was, but to hold up a mirror, revealing how wonderful we can be. I felt on a much deeper level what he was saying. Walk on the water, Peter. Why do you doubt? (Matthew 14:29). Greater works than this shall you do, if only you believe (John 14:11–12). Believe in yourself. Remember who you are.

I've learned that being perfect has nothing to do with how many mistakes we make. In fact there actually are no mistakes when I realize the perfection in the entire process. And the process is about finding completeness and enjoying the journey all along the way. We are only here to experience and learn. Therein lies the perfection. There is less to do and far more to be. Simply look to the light and blossom. "Consider the lilies of the field, how they grow; they do not toil, neither do they spin . . . [yet] Solomon in all his glory was not arrayed like one of [them]" (Matthew 6:28–29). We are the lilies. We are the beautiful manifestations of everything divine, simply growing and pointing upward toward home.

The Olsen family

I've learned that our individual healing is up to us. When we decide to heal emotionally, we will. Family, friends, strangers, even angels will assist us along the way, but our wholeness in the end is dependent upon our willingness to receive it.

"Physician, heal thyself" (Luke 4:23). "Thy faith has made thee whole" (Luke 17:19).

I've learned that true joy comes through the simple things in life—the way my wife's toes touch my leg under the covers in the morning, feeling the laughter of my sons, buying an eight-dollar hummingbird feeder. Looking for happiness in big things usually leaves me empty, while embracing life's beautiful, little miracles fills my heart with gratitude.

I've learned that faith and hope can literally be transformed into absolute trust. When the rug is completely yanked out from under you, and everything you hoped for, everything you had faith in, vanishes, leaving only trust. Trust that God will walk with you through the darkness. When hope and faith are waning, we are in our most beautiful state. It is the state that brings about perfect love, complete trust. Remember faith, hope, and charity, "but the greatest of these is charity," perfect love (1 Corinthians 13:13).

We come from perfect love and we will return to it someday, but for now we get to love imperfectly here. Beautifully flawed in this lower dimension, we simply do our best. We learn from our choices, getting up each time we fall. The skinned knees and

Jeff and Tonya

106

scraped palms are not signs of our shame, but rather badges of our courage for having come to play the game. We are the noble and great ones. Like shattered pots artistically reassembled, we are beautiful in our brokenness. Perfection actually lives within the chaos. Everything is in divine order regardless of the judgments we put on it. We are in very good hands.

Exhale.

Trust, live, love, laugh, cry, heal, awaken, and choose joy as we stumble along our perfect path.

∞ = Infinity

◯ = Eternity

MILE
8
0

afterword

My father taught me about mile markers when I was a young girl. We traveled the open road often. I can still remember asking, "Daddy, what do all those signs with numbers mean?"

"Sweetheart," he replied, "those numbers are mile markers, and they are there if you lose your way. They help you find your way home."

Jeff's book *Beyond Mile Marker 80* reminds us that every day of life is a sacred gift and an opportunity to discover the miracle of what lies "beyond mile marker 80." His remarkable journey will touch your heart as he shares all that came before and after his "mile-marker moment" in the most inspiring way.

Each new day provides us with opportunities to develop the courage to open the book of our deepest trials. Rumi said, "The wound is the place where the light enters you." It requires extraordinary courage to travel to our deepest wounds within, yet when we do, we discover our own personal truth, and it is that truth that ultimately sets us free.

We come to understand that, like everything else in life, trials pass and we naturally grow wiser from the knowledge we gained in the experience. In his first book, *I Knew Their Hearts*, Jeff writes about the great challenges he faced with the accident that killed his wife and son and left him seriously injured. He endured with humility these seasons in his life, and his heart grew strong and soft beyond measure. When his autumn season came—a season every bit as breathtaking as spring—he discovered his wife Tonya, his "beyond mile marker 80" miracle. I have never met Tonya, yet in reading Jeff's words I grew to deeply and profoundly love and respect her.

Jeff reminds us that we can discover our personal "mile marker 80" (MM80) miracles when our hearts are open and willing. After reading Jeff's book, I had the opportunity to travel the path of the actual mile marker that Jeff speaks of in his book. I turned off my cell phone, my radio, and the city. And in the quiet, I let the mile markers drive my heart with no expectations.

Following Jeff's example, I summoned the courage to look deep within my heart and finally pull out all my "rocks" (trials, challenges, and judgments) that had accumulated through my lifetime and return them to the road.

MM12—I gave up the rock of trying so hard to be perfect all the time.

MM13—I gave up the rock of unkind judgments from others that I have buried within.

MM14—I forgave myself for the times when I was unkind.

MM15—I asked for forgiveness in requiring others to be perfect.

Each mile marker was a mirror that reflected back to me what I was unnecessarily holding on to so I could then find the strength to let go.

MM80—This was a most sacred ground, a place where Jeff's heart and life were shattered. I didn't stop because those lessons and journeys belong to Jeff and his family. I simply offered a humble and simple prayer to respect all that had come before.

MM81—I began to feel lighter. All the heavy rocks in my heart were gone. A small whisper arose, saying, "It's okay for you to be happy." I smiled and kept driving. I rolled down the window and breathed fresh winter air deep into my lungs. I felt peaceful, happy and uplifted. I remembered Jeff's words, "Exhale. Trust, live, love, laugh, cry, heal, awaken, and choose joy as we stumble along our perfect path."

Until that moment, my path had felt so far from perfect. Jeff assisted me to discover that my path was indeed perfect for me and in that moment I truly became light in my heart. There were no heavy rocks in there to weigh me down.

When I returned home, I called my father. "What's up, sweetheart?" he asked. "Are you okay?"

"Yes, Dad. I just wanted to call and say I love you."

"I know, honey."

"Do you remember teaching me about the mile markers when I was a little girl?"

"Yes, honey," he replied.

"I finally understand what you were trying to teach me so I wouldn't lose my way in life."

"You can always find your way home by following the mile markers," he said—just like he had said all those years ago. I smiled and knew that the mile markers are truly unconditional love, and with love in our hearts we can always find our way home.

—*Mary Michelle Scott*

President, Fishbowl
Contributor to *Forbes* and *Harvard Business Review*

If you have been touched by the message of this book and wish to continue the conversation, feel free to contact me at

www.atonenow.com

about the author

$\mathcal{J}$*effery Olsen* is a talented mentor, consultant, author, and inspirational speaker.

In 1997, Jeff experienced a horrific automobile accident that inflicted multiple life-threatening injuries, including crushing both his legs. His left leg was amputated above the knee. The most devastating outcome of the accident was the loss of his wife and youngest son, who were both killed instantly. At that time, Jeff had a profound near-death experience that deepened his spirituality and gave him insights and gifts not common in today's world. Having that glimpse into heaven gave him courage to carry on, heal, and care for his living son. He has since remarried and adopted two more boys.

Professionally, Olsen brings soul and an invigorating work ethic to everything he does. He has been internationally decorated for his creative work and has appeared in *Forbes*. With accolades from the Clio Awards, the One Show, Communication Arts, and the National ADDYs, Jeff takes his place among the linchpins of his industry. Jeff's greatest joy, however, comes from simply being a husband, father, and friend. He participates in speaking tours and conferences where he shares deep spiritual insights based on his incredible life experiences. *Beyond Mile Marker 80* is his second book, a sequel to *I Knew Their Hearts*. Find out more about Jeff at his website, www.atonenow.com.

FOREWORD BY DR. RAYMOND MOODY

i knew their hearts

JEFF OLSEN

THE AMAZING TRUE STORY OF A JOURNEY
BEYOND THE VEIL TO LEARN THE SILENT
LANGUAGE OF THE HEART

i knew their hearts

After a tragic accident took the life of his wife and son, Jeff experienced a miracle. This personal and poignant journey into the life after death shares the true story of Jeff's out-of-body experiences and his newly remembered ability to communicate at a deeper level with people on both sides of the veil. It's a moving read you won't want to miss!

0 26575 13989 1